D1265219

THE ALTERNATIVE INFLUENCE

The Impact of Investigative Reporting Groups on America's Media

Philip F. Lawler

MERCYHURST COLLEGE LIBRARY
ERIE, PA. 16546

UNIVERSITY
PRESS OF
AMERICA

LANHAM • NEW YORK • LONDON

the
media
institute

Copyright © 1984 by

The Media Institute

University Press of America,™ Inc.

4720 Boston Way
Lanham, MD 20706

3 Henrietta Street
London WC2E 8LU England

All rights reserved

Printed in the United States of America

Library of Congress Cataloging in Publication Data

Lawler, Philip F.
  The alternative influence.

  1. Mass media—United States—Objectivity.
2. Journalism—United States—Objectivity. I. Title.
P96.0242U64 1984   302.2'34'0973   84-15274
ISBN 0-8191-4233-6 (alk. paper)
ISBN 0-8191-4234-4 (pbk.: alk. paper)

Co-published by arrangement with
The Media Institute

All University Press of America books are produced on acid-free
paper which exceeds the minimum standards set by the National
Historical Publications and Records Commission.

Table of Contents

Acknowledgment

Mr. Lawler and The Media Institute wish to acknowledge Mr. James Bovard, a free-lance journalist, whose preliminary research on this topic was of great value.

Introduction

Investigative journalism is arduous, controversial, and—most of all—expensive. A reporter who embarks on a major investigation must face the possibility that the well will prove dry, or that sources will be too recalcitrant to provide reliable information. Even if the investigation proceeds apace, the writer might find few publishers willing to print a very hot story. To overcome these hurdles, a number of individuals have banded together in consortia of investigative journalists, and a number of institutions have devoted their resources to the support of this work. This book focuses on nine such organizations, whose histories are sketched in the first chapter.

The organizations in question are neither large nor powerful, yet they do wield a demonstrable influence over the larger organs of the major media—and thus over the whole of American public opinion. The secrets of their success provide an intriguing set of insights into the way American journalism is constituted today—the techniques of reporting, the weaknesses and foibles of large media outlets, and the editorial judgments that color all our news.

These nine organizations were selected—and others excluded—for this study by a set of criteria that warrants explanation. This is not simply a book about investigative reporting. That would be a very worthwhile topic in itself (if anyone could define the term "investigative reporting" adequately). But this book pursues a more restricted topic. There are hundreds or thousands of reporters in this country who claim to be doing investigative work. And there are dozens of organizations that support that work. But there are very few organizations that push investigative journalism to the forefront of their activities. The organizations surveyed in this book are among those few, unusual institutions.

This book is not a work of investigative reporting. Of the material presented here, almost all is available to the public in published form; the remainder was obtained by a simple process of interviewing interested parties. The purpose of this book is not to uncover new facts, nor to unmask corruption in high places, but simply to appraise the life of the American mass media from one very specialized angle. What follow are reflections on a phenomenon that, while it is very rarely noticed, exercises a strong and growing influence on American journalism.

Among the numerous groups active in American journalism, only a handful make investigative journalism their purpose. Most reporters make their careers in traditional newspaper, magazine, or broadcast journalism. Those who choose to concentrate exclusively on investigations, without establishing a firm base at some media outlet, obviously have special motives for their decision. What, exactly, are those motives? And what sort of motives bind the investigators who band together to pool their talents? The investigative-reporting organizations surely follow a set of dictates unlike those that guide ordinary newsmen. In fact, the approach of these organizations to journalism is even quite different from that of investigative reporters outside these few special organizations. In a word, the organizations portrayed in this book constitute a unique aspect of American reporting today.

Yet these organizations, although they are small in number and in size, can have a marked impact on the shaping of public opinion. Because their work is so little noticed—because so few people are aware of their existence—their influence has never been assessed. This book offers a preliminary appraisal of that influence, and of the means by which it is exerted. Investigative reporting enjoys a particular vogue today, and perhaps the problems posed by these reporting organizations highlight the problems of the larger world of journalism.

One of the most cherished tenets of American journalism is the belief that a reporter should follow his story wherever it may lead. And one of the basic facts of life in any profession—including journalism—is that competition breeds excellence. So reporters should be not only aggressive in searching out facts, but also competitive in seeking to tell the story better than their competitors. Yet somehow reporters rarely spend their investigative energies on each other; newspapers do not often feature critiques of their rivals. Since the mass media today constitute a powerful social institution, it would seem only natural that investigative reporters would devote some attention to journalism itself. But they do not. Why do they avoid that topic? And why do they choose other topics? These questions are cast in sharp relief when one observes organized investigators at work.

Whatever motivates an independent investigator, his work is fruitless unless he can convince someone to publish it. So the relationships between independent investigators and established journalists are charged with a special significance. The investigators cannot survive without help from their cousins in the established journals; that should come as no surprise. But perhaps the most interesting aspect of this study is the realization that the mass media lean heavily on the investigators in turn. Each group—investigators and publishers—fills its own role in the process of American journalism. To understand their interactions, and the services they provide each other, is to gain a better understanding of the unspoken laws that guide American journalism today.

The most important result of the investigative work described in this book is the influence it exerts on the editorial judgment of "main line" journalists. If investigative organizations can convince media outlets to report on their findings, then these organizations have in effect turned the mass media into their own publicists.

One of the groups discussed herein, the Center for Investigative Reporting, in its promotional brochure quotes Bob Maynard, editor and publisher of the *Oakland Tribune*: "It's great having the Center around. It keeps the rest of us on our toes." This book is dedicated to the proposition that someone should keep the Center, and its cousins, on their toes as well.

Chapter I: Investigative Reporting Groups

An investigative-reporting *organization* differs significantly from a publication that sponsors and/or uses investigative reports. Every daily newspaper includes the product of reporters' investigations. Many magazines, too, look for articles that shed new light into dark corners. Some journals provide special funding for such articles, enabling writers to devote an unusual amount of time and to incur a heavy set of expenses in the search for a reportorial jackpot. However, aside from *Mother Jones* and *Reason* magazines (described below), no major publication makes investigative journalism its *raison d'etre*. Unlike the publications in which their work occasionally appears, the organizations described below are notable because they initiate investigations in furtherance of the cause of investigative journalism.

Better Government Association

Fairly or unfairly, the city of Chicago has acquired an unmatched reputation as a haven for mobsters and political connivers. So perhaps it is fitting that Chicago is also the home of the oldest, best known, and most successful organization devoted to investigative journalism. In 1923, at the height of Chicago's battle against organized crime, the Anti-Saloon Temperance League spun off the Better Government Association.[1] At first the Better Government Association (BGA) concentrated on the abundant problems of the Capone era. But within a decade the organization had entered the political arena proper, rating candidates for public office.

During the 1960s, Chicago's political history again wrought a major change in the organization. As the Democratic party machine of Richard Daley grew in power and influence, the BGA joined forces with dissident Democrats and with Republicans led by Charles Percy in "Operation Watchdog," and began to undertake dramatic undercover investigations to expose corruption within the city's machinery. The campaign brought new laurels to the BGA, most notably when a BGA investigation led to the political demise of Mayor Daley's right-hand man, Chicago alderman Tom Keane.[2]

BGA investigations were not confined to Chicago alone, however. Investigations also proceeded into Medicaid fraud, the Federal Railroad Administration, Pentagon contracts, the Small Business Administration, the Farm Loan Program, and even government "spying" on U.S. citizens. As this book is being written, Congressional committees in Washington are plowing through a mound of information involving corruption in Navy shipbuilding contracts—information unearthed primarily through the efforts of the BGA.[3]

In its years of successful muckraking, the BGA has developed a consistent *modus operandi*. When suspicious facts come to light, the BGA brings in a partner: a newspaper or television station that takes part in the investigation, and publicizes the findings of the investigative team. So time after time, BGA reports capture headlines. Nor is the BGA content simply to dramatize its allegations of corruption. Once the investigation is complete, BGA participants often visit Washington (or, if it is a local matter, the Illinois Capitol at Springfield) to testify on the possibilities for effective reform. The BGA emphasizes its commitment to what its name implies: better government. Advocating improved regulations, or suggesting more efficient approaches to public policy, is thus an integral part of the organization's work.

Founded nearly a half-century before its competitors, the BGA had built a formidable reputation, and a substantial financial base, before investigative reporting returned to vogue in the mid-'70s. Still, regardless of its many past successes, BGA officials look upon 1977 as the organization's best year. In 1977, acting in concert with reporters from the *Chicago Sun-Times*, BGA investigators bought, renovated, and operated the Mirage, a bar on Chicago's North Side. There, unwitting city officials solicited bribes while hidden cameras rolled and incriminating evidence mounted. When the Mirage story was published (and broadcast on *60 Minutes*), the reverberations were powerful; over 100 indictments were eventually handed down.[4]

That rousing success alone would have made 1977 a banner year for the BGA, but more was to come. In 1979 the MacArthur Foundation, a Chicago-based charitable trust, announced an award of $500,000 to the BGA, renewable for five years—a total gift of $2.5 million.[5] That windfall boosted the BGA budget to over $1 million annually.[6] Foundation and corporate grants, investment income, and membership dues paid by the BGA's individual and corporate supporters provide the organization's revenues; only a small trickle of income is generated directly by BGA investigations.

In the course of its 60 years of muckraking, the BGA has earned the wrath of both major political parties, and innumerable factions and interest groups. During the early 1970s, Mayor Daley charged that the organization was working in cahoots with the Republicans—a charge made less plausible by the fact that Governor James Thompson, Daley's chief Republican adversary, insisted that the BGA was in the Democratic camp.[7] Over the years, such charges have balanced themselves out, so that today the BGA can take up promising investigations without fear of being accused of ideological or political motives.

Because of its insistence on ideological neutrality, the BGA cannot count on the appeal of participation in a political movement as a recruiting device. But apparently recruiting is not a problem. When the BGA opened a Washington office for the first time in 1979 (as a result of the MacArthur grant), 600 candidates applied for six research positions.[8] The BGA pay scale is decent but not overwhelming; investigators receive salaries ranging from $15,000 to $20,000.[9] The work can be painstaking—when it involves long searches through public records—or exciting—when it reaches its climax in public revelations. At times, there must be an element of personal danger, since BGA investigators occasionally carry concealed cameras or tape recorders to their undercover assignments with some unsavory characters. To preserve the secrecy of their investigations, BGA officials insist on confidentiality among their workers; investigators who reveal too much about their work quickly find their jobs in jeopardy.

The majority of BGA staff workers are young college graduates from somewhere in the general vicinity of Chicago. Many come from law schools, some from political work, and a few have backgrounds in journalism. Virtually none come from partisan political organizations, however, and when they leave the BGA virtually none take positions at such organizations. For most of its young employees, the BGA serves as a stepping stone to a career in related work: journalism, law, or public policy.

BGA investigations have, in recent years, garnered a number of prestigious awards: a National Press Club award for Washington correspondents; the Chicago Newspaper Guild's "Stick-o-Type" award; a UPI award for public service; a National Headliners award; and the Sigma Delta Chi, Peter Lisagor, and Jacob Scher journalism awards.[10] The BGA can also claim at least partial credit for an Emmy Award that went to ABC-TV's *20/20* show on arson—a show prepared in conjunction with a BGA probe.[11]

Younger, less-established organizations would trumpet the news of such awards, but in BGA annual reports they are listed without fanfare. Certainly BGA officials relish the praise their organization receives. But unlike the smaller groups that are struggling to establish a reputation, the BGA already has won national recognition. The BGA board of directors, a sampling of the first rank of Chicago society, tells a story in itself: The BGA is a muckraking organization, yet it is considered eminently respectable nonetheless—a pillar of the Establishment.

Fund for Investigative Journalism

During his years as chairman of the board of the Institute for Policy Studies, a left-wing think tank in Washington, D.C., Philip M. Stern noticed that a steady stream of political activists and journalists came to him with suggestions for investigative projects. Through the Stern Fund, he had the wherewithal to help some of them. But it seemed no established organization existed to receive proposals and make grants for investigative journalism. In 1969, Stern changed all that by setting up the Fund for Investigative Journalism in Washington.[12]

In direct contrast to the BGA, the Fund for Investigative Journalism (FIJ) has no in-house investigative staff. Instead, the Fund provides grants to support free-lance writers in their investigations. The staff consists of one part-time executive director, Howard Bray, a veteran journalist who screens proposals and administers grants.

Ordinarily, FIJ grants are awarded by the organization's board of directors, which meets every few months to consider the proposals that Bray has received. If a project is very timely, and the writer cannot wait for a board meeting, Bray can authorize a small grant himself. Grants are not massive; a typical award might be $500, with only a few special projects receiving more than $1,000. Once the award is given, the rest of the work is the responsibility of the recipient. The Fund endeavors to help make investigative work possible, but offers no editorial nor marketing assistance. This approach enables the FIJ to sponsor a broad array of work on a comparatively small budget. In recent years, the FIJ has awarded roughly 35 grants annually, on a budget of less than $75,000.[13]

The purpose of the FIJ, as expressed in its promotional material, is "increasing public knowledge about the concealed, obscure, or complex aspects of matters significantly affecting the public."[14] Reports backed by FIJ grants, according to the brochure, should be "factual rather than ideological or philosophical."[15] Ordinarily, the FIJ expects the writer's work to appear in a newspaper or magazine; sometimes the work can be expanded into a book. In applying for FIJ support, writers are asked to state where their work will be published, so the Fund can have reasonable assurance that the labor will not be in vain. Writers are also required to see that when their work appears in published form, a credit line acknowledges the help of the FIJ. Occasionally, after dipping into a subject, the recipient of an FIJ grant will discover that his suspicions of corruption were unfounded, and no publishable story will result.

This simple formula has given the Fund for Investigative Journalism an impressive list of publication credits. Articles and columns sponsored by the FIJ have appeared in newspapers such as the London *Times*, *New York Times*, *Washington Post*, *Boston Globe*, *St. Louis Post-Dispatch*, *Chicago Sun-Times*, *Detroit Free Press*, *Newsday*, and countless others; and in an equally wide selection of magazines: *Harper's*, *The Atlantic*, *Nation*, *The Progressive*, *Mother Jones*, *Inquiry*, *Village Voice*, *Washington Monthly*, *Federal Times*, and *New Republic*.[16] Among the books written with FIJ assistance, the best known are Seymour Hersch's *Cover-Up*[17] (an account of the My Lai story), Jessica Mitford's *Cruel and Usual Punishment*,[18] and Victor Marchetti's highly controversial expose, *The CIA and the Cult of Intelligence*.[19] These and other FIJ stories have won two Pulitzer Prizes and numerous awards for journalism.

The FIJ board of directors has sole authority for determining who shall receive FIJ grants. That board currently includes Barbara Cohen, Dorothy Gilliam, Roger Mudd, Roger Wilkins, and Edwin Yoder[20]—all people of some prominence with direct attachments to the world of journalism. While the FIJ does not exercise any editorial control, grantees may consult with members of the FIJ advisory board, including Jack Anderson, Richard Barnet, Carl Bernstein, Seymour Hersch, James J. Kilpatrick, Robert Novak, James Ridgeway, Eileen Shanahan, Philip Stern, and Bob Woodward.[21]

Despite the organization's professed disdain for "ideological or philosophical" work,[22] it is worth noting that virtually all of those listed above (with Edwin Yoder, James Kilpatrick, and Robert Novak the notable exceptions) belong somewhere on the liberal side of the political spectrum. Similarly, the list of publications in which FIJ work has appeared runs from the political center leftward. Executive director Howard Bray professes some concern about this fact; he hopes to see more FIJ credits in conservative journals, and points to an FIJ piece in *National Review* as a model.[23] But that grant was made in 1976, and no new conservative publications have been added to the FIJ list of credits.

Because the FIJ accomplishes so much on so small a budget, and because its credit line is seen so frequently, the Fund has a comparatively easy time maintaining its finances. Each year, several foundations provide grants of a few thousand dollars to the FIJ, and the investment of the FIJ's endowment brings in several thousand dollars more. With this revenue, the Fund is able to support the projects approved by its board—roughly one-third of those submitted for consideration.

Pacific News Service

In 1970, the Institute for Policy Studies (the left-wing think tank) founded a subsidiary organization on the West Coast. This new organization, called the Bay Area Institute, in turn gave birth to the Pacific News Service, a syndication service for the written product of a new breed of journalists.[24] Each week, the Pacific News Service (PNS) sent out five mailings to newspapers that subscribed to its service, offering them eight "news analysis" articles that ranged from 800 to 1,200 words in length. PNS terms were attractive; as late as 1978, the syndicate charged only $15 per month for a small-town weekly newspaper, or up to $100 for a large urban daily.[25]

The price was right, and the columns were lively. But the results were not impressive. For several years, PNS labored in obscurity, its budget always in jeopardy. In retrospect, that lack of success is easily explained: most non-ideological publications considered the PNS material too controversial, too blatantly left of center.

To be sure, in the early 1970s PNS was offering stories that were not available elsewhere. For instance, a PNS correspondent was the last American to leave Cambodia in 1975.[26] But the flavor of the stories was a bit too strong. As the *Columbia Journalism Review* noted in an October 1978 article, those reports from Cambodia "consistently challenged U.S. press accounts of Khmer Rouge brutality."[27] Even the editor of *In These Times*, the national socialist weekly (which, by the way, is also subsidized by the Institute for Policy Studies), chided PNS for its reliance on leftist writers.[28]

By the time the PNS correspondent left Cambodia, the syndicate was already taking steps to shuck off its radical image. The change in tone was dictated by the marketplace. PNS had never enjoyed a large regular clientele, and the list of subscribers hovered around 50 at best. By 1974, the syndicate had lost its last daily subscriber.[29] In April 1974, PNS had appointed a new managing editor, Alexandra Close, under whose tutelage the syndicate would revive dramatically.

Coming to PNS from her post as China editor for the *Far East Economic Review*, Close had some acquaintance with mainstream publications, and some knowledge of how they select their material. She toned down the ideological content of the PNS columns, and broadened the syndicate's appeal by adding domestic political stories to the usual complement of foreign news coverage. At the same time, she set out on a vigorous fundraising campaign to find operating revenue. Her work was rewarded; the number of PNS subscribers climbed steadily.

The first major breakthrough for PNS came in 1977, when the Markle Foundation provided a $35,000 grant for marketing and promotion of PNS syndication services.[30] By the end of that same year, the number of subscribers had jumped from 90 to over 200.[31] With a potential audience of something like seven million readers, PNS now reached a major national audience. Close parlayed that new prominence into more fundraising success, and the syndicate's income soared. In 1976, PNS revenue had been $115,000; in 1977, it was $197,000, and in 1978, $209,000.[32] And even those figures may be artificially low; in 1978 PNS also began work on a $90,000 special project which the Ford Foundation had awarded to PNS co-founder Franz Schurmann—a grant that did not officially come through PNS and therefore did not appear on its books.[33]

Still, the best was yet to come. In 1981, the *Christian Science Monitor*, which had been offering syndicated stories through the *Des Moines Register and Tribune*, switched to the *Washington Post/Los Angeles Times* syndicate. Looking for a substitute to fill out its offerings, the *Des Moines Register and Tribune* spotted PNS—a lively, unusual service whose nonprofit status made its rates unusually low. The marriage was soon consummated. Today, *Register and Tribune* officials estimate that about 175 papers use PNS stories.[34] In any case, PNS stories go out over the wire regularly (saving PNS the considerable costs of twice-weekly mass mailings), and are used by such newspapers as the *Washington Post, Los Angeles Times, Boston Globe, Chicago Tribune, Baltimore Sun, Miami Herald, Atlanta Journal, Cleveland Plain Dealer*, and *Philadelphia Inquirer*.[35]

Flushed with success, PNS also set up a special service for radio news organizations. "Rip 'n' Read," as it was known, provided about a dozen stories *daily* for its subscribers, each one tightly worded to fit radio news formats. By 1981, Rip 'n' Read had over 300 radio stations subscribing to its services.[36] At that point, however, Rip 'n' Read separated from PNS, forming its own corporate identity.

The Pacific News Service under Alexandra Close has softened its editorial bias considerably, so that only a careful reader notices the underlying ideological bias. One admirer, the managing editor of the Sunday *Boston Globe*, told the *Columbia Journalism Review* in 1978:

> When PNS was an alternative kind of thing that was heavily into Vietnam, there were some editors at the *Globe* who grew rather nervous about it as an objective, dispassionate service. For a few years, we didn't do any business at all to speak of. But beginning about three years ago [that is, when Close took control], I became impressed with what seemed to me to be substantive, important reporting on a wide variety of subjects which clearly had no ideological bias.[37]

PNS denies that it has any ideological bias at all. The preferred term, used in all PNS literature, is "thinking journalism."[38] But this "thinking journalism" has, at the very least, a peculiar pattern. The *Register and Tribune* syndicate brochure says that "PNS has a deliberate global perspective."[39] What is that perspective? Alexandra Close explains that "we look for people who are really steeped in their areas, people who have time to think."[40] The result is a sort of journalism that looks into the future. "When you put trends together, rather than isolating them, you get very exciting patterns," she told the *Columbia Journalism Review*.[41]

The "very exciting patterns" are themselves identified in the PNS publicity brochure. In fact, the brochure's explication of "thinking journalism" is worth an extended quotation:

> PNS believes that a major change is taking place in the world: People, independent of governments, are acting on their own to secure their survival, to create hope for themselves and their children. Their cumulative decisions are reshaping the world as we know it—through vast global migrations, religious revolutions, burgeoning alternative economies. To cover these changes, PNS starts at the ground level—the chicken's-eye view—and moves from the bottom up rather than the top down. Instead of depending on government handouts or academic sources for explanations, we bring scholars, reporters and thinkers together to deal with what often are the least known, least understood emerging news stories.[42]

In line with this operating philosophy, PNS often uses stories that look upon contemporary political problems from the viewpoint of a single citizen—either in the United States or abroad. This technique enables the writer to convey a special perspective without uncovering his own political preferences. The typical PNS story does not involve investigative journalism, strictly speaking. Rather, it involves the use of unusual approaches to news stories. True to their words, PNS writers refuse to accept the facts and explanations that come from standard news sources.

Operating out of a cramped, cluttered office suite near San Francisco's convention center, PNS works with a stable of regular contributors, supplementing their work with material submitted by outside academics and free-lance writers. To anyone working with PNS, the appeal lies in potential readership rather than financial reward. Writers receive only $50 for an article, and even full-time staff workers earn considerably less than $20,000 annually.[43] In 1978, after her year of signal success in marketing the syndicate and raising new revenues, Alexandra Close rewarded herself with a salary *cut*—from $9,622 to $7,766.70.[44] PNS staffers obviously feel they are working for a cause.

Mother Jones

In 1976, the Institute for Policy Studies set up the Foundation for National Progress in San Francisco. Papers filed with the California Secretary of State explained that the new foundation's "specific and primary purpose is to carry out on the West Coast the charitable and educational activities of the Institute for Policy Studies."[45] Almost immediately, the Foundation for National Progress began publishing a glossy monthly magazine entitled *Mother Jones*.

Mother Jones, so named after the legendary union organizer Mary Harris "Mother" Jones, made no bones about its radical politics. Early issues praised Fidel Castro, and expressed open satisfaction with the military victories of the North Vietnamese. But gradually, the editorial emphasis changed, and strident propaganda was replaced by an emphasis on muckraking and debunking. In particular, the magazine emphasized investigations of major American corporations. "We see it as MJ's special task," a 1978 editorial explained, "to inaugurate the era of corporate exposes. After all, corporations and their products hold far greater sway over our lives than do politicians."[46]

The change brought new respectability; in its first full year of publication (1977), an article entitled "A Case of Corporate Malpractice" was a finalist in the National Magazine Award competition.[47] With this new respectability came new readership. By 1983 *Mother Jones* had received three National Magazine Awards. *Mother Jones* grew in size and in circulation, and today reaches about 200,000 subscribers.[48] That figure represents a truly stunning achievement for a magazine devoted to political affairs. Both *New Republic* and *National Review*, the primary journals of liberal and conservative ideas respectively, hover slightly under 100,000 in circulation.[49]

More to the point, neither *New Republic* nor *National Review* is published by a nonprofit corporation. The tax exemption that *Mother Jones* enjoys through the Foundation for National Progress provides the magazine with a huge advantage, particularly in nonprofit postage costs. For magazines of this size, which aggresively seek to increase circulation, a very large expense is the cost of recruiting new subscribers. And the largest portion of that cost, in turn, is usually the postage required for mass mailings to thousands of potential subcribers. *Mother Jones* has a large competitive advantage over its rivals, then—an advantage estimated at $200,000, which has not escaped the notice of the Internal Revenue Service. Starting in 1980, when a seemingly routine IRS audit raised questions about the magazine's right to tax-exempt status, *Mother Jones* became embroiled in a running controversy to preserve its exemption. To date, the magazine's struggle has been successful, with the IRS deciding in November 1983 that *Mother Jones* is, indeed, entitled to its tax exemption.

IRS willing, *Mother Jones* can continue to make ends meet with the income generated by advertisements, subscription income, and a subsidy from the Foundation for National Progress that might be much larger (funds permitting) were it not for the magazine's postage break. At $12, the cost of a year's subscription is a bargain, and apparently the *Mother Jones* promotion department has found the audience that responds to the magazine's appeal. Each issue advertises a further inducement to boost circulation: if a subscriber donates one-half the cost of a gift subscription for his local library, the Foundation for National Progress makes up the remainder.

Who are the readers of *Mother Jones*? The Carter White House received and monitored the magazine. Presumably, however, the editors have an accurate portrait of their more typical subscribers. In a May 1982 piece, executive editor Deirdre English provided some clues:

> Today, the Left—defined as a broad amalgam, including many feminists, environmentalists, racial and ethnic minorities, progressive labor leaders, community activists, antiwar and antinuclear crusaders and so forth—is reawakening, shaken by the nightmare of the Reagan regime. The rebellious and utopian spirit of the 60s will be a powerful ingredient in the political admixture of the 80s—just watch.[50]

Center for Investigative Reporting

The Fund for Investigative Journalism, Pacific News Service, and *Mother Jones* formed a powerful team. Yet in 1977, the Stern Fund provided money to help launch still another California organization, the Center for Investigative Reporting.[51] The three co-founders of the new organization were veterans of the alternative media: Lowell Bergman, from the *San Diego Street Journal*, and Daniel Noyes and David Weir from *Rolling Stone*. The Center for Investigative Reporting was to be a journalistic cooperative, enabling individual writers to undertake the costs of long, in-depth investigations by sharing those costs with other journalists under a tax-exempt umbrella.

The three main actors in the new corporation came to the CIR with their reputations for investigative work already established. Lowell Bergman was described in a *Mother Jones* piece (written by his colleague David Weir) as "one of the best investigative reporters in the country."[52] Noyes and Weir had led a special investigative-reporting squad at *Rolling Stone*. Noyes and Weir were also members of the "Phoenix Project" team that earned fame in probing organized crime in Arizona.[53]

In spite of their reputations, the CIR team members suffered through the same financial crises that had marked the early days of the other organizations in their field. Looking back on those trials from the comparative security of 1981, Weir told an *Oakland Tribune* reporter, "There was a time there when we'd get the next dollar just in time to continue for a few more weeks. Sometimes we'd go on half salary just to keep going."[54] But the CIR did survive, placing articles in left-oriented publications such as *Mother Jones, New West*, and *The Progressive*. That, together with grants income, held the CIR together through its first few years. According to one 1981 account, the list of foundations supporting the CIR included the Playboy, Norman, and Tides Foundations, Greenpeace, the Fund for Constitutional Government, Warsh-Mott Fund, Gannett Newspaper Foundation, and the National Council of Churches.[55] Then, too, there are two more familiar names: The Fund for Investigative Journalism and the Pacific News Service are also said to have provided financial assistance to the CIR.[56]

Then, in 1980, lightning struck. A CIR article in *Mother Jones* won the National Magazine Award from the Columbia School of Journalism and National Council of Magazine Editors.[57] Instantly, the CIR had won respectability. As the *Oakland Tribune* put it, the award "attracted the financial support of a number of foundations that didn't give them a second look" in their trying early days.[58] As of 1981 the CIR budget was hovering around the $150,000 mark annually— about half of it furnished by foundation grants.[59]

The next big break for the CIR came when the organization began to cultivate ties with major television networks. In 1978, ABC-TV hired Lowell Bergman away from the CIR to work with its investigating team for *20/20*; he was quickly promoted to coordinate ABC investigations. In August 1983 he moved again, becoming a producer on CBS' *60 Minutes*. Perhaps Bergman was instrumental in assigning the CIR the task of researching a *20/20* story in 1980 on fundraising abuses in the International Year of the Child. The project was a success from all perspectives, and soon the CIR signed an agreement to work steadily with ABC on *20/20* stories.[60] CBS saw the virtues of such an arrangement, as well, and in February 1982 *60 Minutes* featured a CIR story called "The Bad Drug: Selacryn." Again, the experiment was a success, and the CIR won a contract to work regularly with *60 Minutes*.[61] The massive viewing audiences commanded by these television shows dwarf the readership of the CIR's usual print outlets, and multiply the organization's effectiveness.

The courtship with television apparently cost the CIR some of the time it might have devoted to published work. In 1980, despite the additional resources made available by the National Magazine Award, the total list of CIR publications declined to four, compared with 14 in 1979.[62] But by 1981 the CIR had adjusted to its dual role as provider of both print and video investigations; 11 articles appeared.[63] Still more important, the 1981 product appeared in a broader array of publications: the *Columbia Journalism Review*, *Los Angeles Times*, *California Living*, and *Inquiry* were added to the list along with the old standbys *Mother Jones*, *New West*, and the IPS-supported socialist weekly, *In These Times*.[64]

Officers of the CIR are relatively ill paid, with full-time salaries ranging well below $20,000.[65] The CIR was originally set up because, as Mark Dowie of *Mother Jones* put it, "Here's a small group of people who would otherwise be starving as free-lancers, getting together to support themselves in a profession that just isn't very viable."[66]

Does it work? The CIR as an institution has acquired a reputation much greater than its individual staff members could have earned independently. Yet the total published product of the Center has never been overwhelming: an average output of a dozen articles each year.[67] Since at any given time there have been roughly a dozen writers affiliated with the CIR, the "cooperative" advantage is invisible. Consider, too, that some of the articles listed in CIR compilations were not actually written by CIR personnel, but simply supported by grants from the CIR.[68] And the articles generally appeared in a relatively small number of publications, with a readership covering only a narrow segment of the political spectrum.[69]

It has been the CIR's venture into television which has accounted for most of the group's recent success. But the CIR lost something in joining forces with the major national networks; the CIR byline is gone, replaced by a fleeting credit squeezed in before a commercial break. For that price, however, CIR investigators can send their messages to an audience incalculably larger than the one they reach through the print medium.

CIR stories follow the same themes stressed by *Mother Jones*, even when they do not appear in that magazine. The CIR frequently looks for corruption and fraud in the corporate world, with a special emphasis on environmental concerns. The workings of the federal government are probed most vigorously in the realm of national defense. Two of the CIR's best-known projects illustrate those special concerns. The story that won the National Magazine Award, an expose on pesticide exports, grew eventually into a book: *Circle of Poison*, by David Weir and Mark Schapiro.[70] David Kaplan's "Where the Bombs Are" alleged that the Navy routinely transports nuclear warheads through public areas, including San Francisco Bay.[71] In each case, the CIR's charges provoked a chorus of protests, calls for investigations, and even hearings in the U.S. Congress and the UN.[72] So those articles fulfilled the CIR's purpose as it is described in the organization's 1980-81 compendium: "At its best, investigative reporting can inform the citizenry, providing the facts needed for active participation in society" (although the author found the CIR less than eager to "inform the citizenry" about its own affairs).[73] To date, CIR studies may not have changed U.S. public policy on any major issue. But with the growing television audience the CIR can now reach, its influence might grow.

Investigative Resource Center

Late in 1977, the North American Congress on Latin America closed down its West Coast office, leaving an extensive library of books, magazines, and clippings critical of U.S. policies in Central America. That collection became the intellectual capital of another new organization, the Investigative Resource Center. In time, the original collection would be complemented by books and magazines donated by other libraries: colleges in the area, friendly organizations, and—that name again—the Stern Fund.[74] Gradually, the Investigative Resource Center (IRC) fleshed out its collection to cover not only Latin America, but the whole gamut of public policy. The IRC now has a collection of some 3,500 books, directories, and government documents; 400 periodicals, including a number of obscure "progressive" journals; and a massive set of thousands upon thousands of press clippings, which literally spill out of the drawers and boxes lining the IRC's densely packed Oakland offices.[75]

Shortly after its inception, the IRC split into two operating divisions: the Information Service on Latin America and the Data Center. The Information Service on Latin America, borne out of the parent North American Congress on Latin America, provides subscribers with an exhaustive set of some 450-500 press clippings every month, culled from the most influential newspapers in the English-speaking world: the *New York Times, Washington Post, Wall Street Journal, Christian Science Monitor, Los Angeles Times, Miami Herald, Financial Times* of London, *Journal of Commerce*, and the weekly *Manchester Guardian/Le Monde*. For an annual fee of $390, subscribers may receive the full 300-page monthly mailing.[76] The Service also provides smaller, less-expensive mailings about individual countries or blocs of countries within Latin America, and microfilmed versions of the same clippings for those interested. Subscribers include embassies and universities, scholars and human-rights activists, corporations, unions, and churches.[77]

The Data Center offers a roughly similar product for a much broader audience. Simply put, the Data Center is a reference library; but it is a library of a very unusual sort. A staff of 10 people, aided by a handful of volunteers and student interns, helps Data Center users seek out the information they need on individuals, organizations, and corporations active within the political sphere. The library collection itself is helpful, especially for someone looking for smaller, more polemical journals. But the greatest attraction, for most users, is the clipping collection and the people who guide visitors through it. Data Center staffers provide assistance to all who want it, regardless of age, political preferences, or ability to pay for their services. Contributions are suggested, but not required, from library users.

This open-door policy matches the avowed political purpose of the IRC. The organization is clearly aligned with "progressive" forces, and expects most of its clients to share its own predilections. The office is run casually, governed by an egalitarian assumption that anyone who seeks the Data Center's help has as much right to be there as anyone else. As the Center's promotional brochure put it, "We provide the tools for labor, community, church, and political organizations working to gain control over their lives."[78]

While the bulk of the Data Center's work comes from various political activists associated with "progressive" causes, the list of those who subscribe to the Center's services is diverse, and includes ABC-TV, the Archdiocese of San Francisco, the *Los Angeles Times*, the Interfaith Center on Corporate Responsibility, the Teamsters Union, and the Corporate Data Exchange.[79] Other investigative organizations also use the IRC regularly (*Mother Jones* is a regular subscriber to the Data Center[80]), and the Center for Investigative Reporting works with the IRC on more than 50 percent of its projects.[81] The Center's 400 subscribers pay $15 apiece ($125 for organizations) annually, and receive a quarterly Data Center newsletter, free research help, cut-rate photocopying, and discounts on publications.[82] The Data Center also reserves some library hours for members only, but during most business hours anyone can walk in off the street and plow through the IRC files.

In addition to its general reference services, the Data Center provides work on contract for interested clients. People who are unable to come to Oakland to use the library can call on IRC staff members to search out data for them, at a modest charge. For a more substantial fee, the IRC will initiate a special search project, compiling clippings on any area the client chooses. This involves searching through the files on hand, rummaging through back issues of relevant publications, organizing the material into a presentable format, and photocopying the result for submission to the client. The cost of this special search service is fixed on a case-by-case basis.

The IRC has already completed some special searches, and offers its products to the general public. There are, for instance, more than 100 "Corporate Profiles" available at $350 apiece. Corporate Profiles include 200 pages of clippings intended to provide the sort of information that does not appear in a company's annual report: "the corporation's social, environmental, and political impact."[83] Culled from 300 periodicals that include both business journals and the socialist bulletins, material in the Corporate Profile includes information on the corporate governance, geographic operations, subsidiaries and products, and relations with consumer groups and labor unions. The IRC pamphlet advertising this service lists the sorts of clients who request Corporate Profiles:

> * a national union... mapping its negotiation strategy against an electronics giant. *an investigative reporter...preparing a

nationwide expose of a secretive construction firm. *a third-world government...renegotiating a contract with a multi-national mining company. *a legal researcher...preparing a wrongful death suit against a chemical corporation. *a public interest group...organizing a national boycott of one of America's largest food processors.[84]

For clients with political interests more general than corporate affairs, the IRC offers a set of several "press profiles" featuring "the best of the press—from daily newspapers, general circulation magazines, religious, labor, and progressive periodicals."[85] These profiles are organized by issue, and include 200-page clip books on: *Reagan's Foreign Policy*, *Reagan and El Salvador*, *The U.S. Military's Game Plan for Asia*, and *Plant Shutdowns: Good Business, Bad News*.[86] In 1981, the IRC produced a poster explaining "Who's Who in the Reagan Administration," listing the professional backgrounds and institutional connections of the top 25 Reagan appointees.[87] The Reagan Administration and its political power base forms the locus of the Data Center's most pressing concern today.

Also in 1981, the Center began producing a series of press profiles that grew into a semi-regular publication, the *New Right Monitor*.[88] At first the project produced two fat volumes entitled *The New Right: Issues and Analyses* and *Fundamentalists and Financiers*.[89] Then there emerged a four-volume work, *The New Right: Readings and Commentary*.[90] Still that was not enough. In the introduction to a fourth publication, condensed from the third, the Data Center's editors explained, "The next right turn points the way toward capturing the House of Representatives and enacting yet more repressive legislation."[91] So the Data Center introduced this volume to "assist progressive organizations and individuals in developing their own social analysis and political strategy to fight the growing threat of the New Right in communities around the country."[92] In 1982, the Center produced two more "updated" versions of the *New Right Monitor*.[93]

Two other IRC projects are worthy of notice. In 1978, the Center helped to organize the Inter-Religious Task Force for Social Analysis, to (in the Center's words) "re-examine the churches' social mission in light of the continuing capitalist crisis."[94] The project produced two publications, entitled *Must We Choose Sides?* and *Which Side Are We On?*, which are advertised as "study/action guides for social change."[95] In 1980, the Center compiled some of its Corporate Profile materials on 300 American corporations to produce a paperbook book, *Everybody's Business, An Almanac: The Irreverent Guide to Corporate America.*[96] Published by Harper & Row, *Everybody's Business* looked critically at corporate labor relations, consumer-safety concerns, and financial practices.

No one could deny that the IRC is fired by ideological beliefs, nor does the Center make any effort to conceal its sympathies. The IRC is, however, careful enough to avoid direct partisan politicking, and so its tax exemption remains intact. Tax-deductible contributions make up a crucial quarter of the annual $150,000 budget,[97] supplementing users' fees, subscription charges, and publication income generated through the activities of the Data Center and the Information Service for Latin America. Recent contributors have included the Ferry and Limantour Funds, and the World Council of Churches.[98]

Fund for Objective News Reporting

The burgeoning growth of the organizations described above might have been expected to provoke some complaints from conservative political operatives. In fact, of course, conservatives had already begun accusing the mass media of harboring a liberal bias. With Vice President Spiro Agnew as the most vociferous press critic, conservative criticisms grew more pronounced during the tumultuous decade of the 1960s. In 1969, the Fund for Objective News Reporting received an endowment of $500,000.[99] Through the 1970s, the Fund (FONR) provided roughly 10 grants each year to conservative writers, enabling them to probe government inefficiencies, foreign powers, and left-wing organizations.[100]

The FONR is guided by a board of directors comprising four well-known conservative journalists: Tom Winter, editor of *Human Events*; Allan Ryskind, Capitol Hill correspondent for the same paper; and syndicated columnists M. Stanton Evans and John Chamberlain.[101] The day-to-day operation of the organization—fielding phone calls, prompting proposals, and keeping the records—is done by an executive director, Clarice Pool. Since the board members (excluding Chamberlain, who is not regularly involved in FONR affairs) all work within a few blocks of each other in Washington, board meetings are informal affairs, held whenever the workload of proposals merits attention.

Like the Fund for Investigative Journalism, the FONR keeps its institutional expenses to a minimum by making grants directly to writers. However, the FONR adds another twist: once the article is finished, it becomes the property of the FONR, to be published at the organization's discretion. So in effect the FONR becomes a sort of literary agent, sending off works to prospective publishers. But the FONR is a very unusual literary agent in one respect: its articles are given to publications free of charge.

Because its generous endowment provides adequate income to sustain regular operations, the FONR does not aggressively seek new sources of income. Working on the interest from its capital, and adding a few outside grants each year, the FONR can afford to commission investigations and pay writers at competitive rates. Payments vary, with the mean somewhere in the vicinity of $1,500, of which half is typically paid in advance to help underwrite the author's expenses. On rare occasions, when an investigation requires major travel expenses, the FONR has provided grants of up to $17,500.[102]

Anyone perusing a list of the projects commissioned by the FONR can detect the institutional bias of the sponsor: The organization is undoubtedly conservative. Recent projects have included studies of the National Endowment for Humanities, the IRS approach to independent contractors, Radio Moscow, Tom Hayden's Campaign for Economic Democracy, the Corporation for Public Broadcasting, and the development of space lasers.[103] One book was produced under FONR auspices: *Missing in Action*,[104] an effort to demonstrate that American GIs are still being held in Vietnam. The authors, too, are identifiably conservative in their orientation. Virtually all grants are given to conservative journalists and activists who are known personally by the board members.

This unabashed ideological slant has one major drawback: most editors are reluctant to use FONR material. Ironically, the fact that FONR articles come free of charge aggravates the problem; editors are suspicious that the material is something akin to a paid political advertisement. So it is not surprising that to date FONR articles have appeared only in publications connected with the conservative political movement. The overwhelming majority have been published in two organs: *National Review* and *Human Events*.[105] Since two members of the FONR board also serve on the *Human Events* editorial team,[106] and two are listed on the *National Review* masthead,[107] the scope of FONR's success is extremely limited.

Within the last year, the FONR has re-oriented its efforts, taking special pains to place its articles in main-line publications such as *Harper's* and *The Atlantic*. To date, there have been no takers. Clarice

Pool, who corresponds with potential publishers, reports that "the rejection letters are generally friendly and encouraging—but they are still rejection letters."[108] To avoid editorial suspicions, the FONR has taken a seemingly perverse step: as an inducement to potential buyers, the FONR has begun requiring payment for its articles. But the lingering identification of the FONR with right-wing causes remains in the minds of the editors Pool approaches. As she also admits, many of the writers working under FONR contracts have not yet adjusted to writing for a broader audience; the articles retain a tendentious ideological style.

Sabre Foundation

Like the Fund for Objective News Reporting, the Sabre Foundation's "investigative journalism fund" represents an effort to counteract liberal bias in the print media. The Sabre Foundation was founded in 1969 as an offshoot of the Ripon Society, but the journalism project was the creation of Mark Frazier, who joined the Sabre Foundation in 1976.[109] Having done a good deal of free-lance writing himself, specializing in government interference with the economic marketplace, Frazier had a keen appreciation of the problems writers faced in preparing and marketing articles in that field. The Sabre program prospectus charged that "journalists have fallen short during recent decades in exercising their watchdog responsibilities."[110]

As the Sabre Foundation saw it, there were marked inefficiencies created by the government, and only a few, relatively impoverished publications willing to tackle the problems. So the Sabre initiative set up a sort of partnership with those publications. Sabre would commission investigative articles on "direct and hidden costs of governmental activities in relation to their benefits."[111] The Sabre fund would pay authors $1,000 for their work, with the understanding that the author would be responsible for arranging publication in one of the cooperating journals.[112] Thus, the journal could have a free story, without sacrificing editorial control.

A number of respected magazines quickly clambered aboard, and became partners with Sabre in the investigative journalism venture. By choice, Sabre limited its offer to journals with a conservative or libertarian flavor—journals that would gratefully accept articles demonstrating government foibles. The participating publications included the *American Spectator*, *Human Events*, *Inquiry*, *Nation*, *New*

Republic, Policy Review, The Progressive, Reason, Ripon Forum, and *Washington Monthly.*[113]

Early reaction to the Sabre support was highly favorable. *New Republic* editor Martin Peretz called it a "splendid and important" initiative.[114] Articles quickly appeared in *Policy Review, Reason,* and *Inquiry* bearing the Sabre credit.[115] Much of the credit for that early success can be attributed directly to the program's director. Technically, all Sabre grants were approved by a board of advisors, but in practice the recruitment and selection of stories was done primarily by Mark Frazier himself.

Working with both editors and writers, and defying some of the normal barriers that separate political ideologies, Frazier constructed a unique alliance. His board of advisors itself was a heterogeneous group: Tom Bethell, James Boyd, John Chamberlain, Steven Chapman, Edith Efron, Michael Novak, Alan Reynolds, William Schulz, Robert Sherrill, and Nicholas von Hoffman—representing publications as different as *National Review* and *The Nation, Reader's Digest* and *Harper's.*[116]

Success, however, was contingent on a single factor: Frazier. The $50,000 budget for the journalism fund[117] represented only a portion of the Sabre Foundation's work, and Frazier's time. Inexorably, as Frazier found other projects—for Sabre and for himself—the journalism initiative suffered the loss of his time and efforts. Whereas at its peak in 1980 the Sabre fund was issuing awards twice annually, and sponsoring 10 projects a year, by 1983 the program had sunk into desuetude.[118] Unable to devote sufficient time to fundraising, and therefore short on cash for grants, the fund now makes its grants only "intermittently," Frazier admits.[119]

Reason

Not too long after his graduation from MIT, where he had prepared for a career in aerospace engineering, Robert Poole realized that his primary interests lay in the realm of political ideas. Specifically, he perceived—and feared—a steady deterioration in the American commitment to individual liberty. The battle to be fought, as he saw it, was a battle of ideas. So his contribution was the creation of a new California-based think tank that would "strengthen the intellectual groundwork for a free society." The Reason Foundation opened its doors in June 1978, assembled an advisory board of prominent economists and philosophers who shared Poole's deep suspicion of government power, and began growing rapidly enough so that the Foundation's budget was projected to hit the $1 million mark in its fifth year of operation.[120]

Steering a careful course between mainstream conservatism and doctrinaire libertarianism, the Reason Foundation has apparently staked out a niche of its own among American think tanks. Its conferences and seminars draw scholars from all over the country, and the Foundation's annual report proudly lists the dozen Reagan Administration officials who have participated actively in Reason Foundation projects.[121] With funding coming from such conservative stalwarts as the Liberty Fund and the Carthage, Earhart, Olin, and Scaife Foundations,[122] and with total gifts still increasing steadily, the Foundation has evidently become a fixture.

The Reason Foundation sponsors a number of different programs, underwriting a host of small publications, and sponsoring several conferences each year. But the flagship publication of the Foundation has always been its monthly journal, *Reason* magazine. And *Reason*, in turn, has from its first issue concentrated primarily on investigative journalism. Following their conviction that government ineptitude can be vividly documented, Poole (who serves as editor) and his staff concentrate on two sorts of investigative work: articles that point out bungling and/or corruption in government programs; and articles that demonstrate efficient ways of solving social problems by voluntary, non-governmental means.

Reason's approach to investigative journalism is roughly similar to that of *Mother Jones*, although the political predilections that guide the two magazines' editors are diametrically opposed. Like *Mother Jones*, *Reason* commissions articles by outside writers, only occasionally publishing investigative work by staff writers. Young free-lancers who share the editorial ideals of the *Reason* staff suggest possibilities, or receive assignments directly from the editors. The painstaking investigative work is done by the writers, who might work on a single investigation for as long as six months. The product is published in *Reason* magazine. While the unpredictable patterns of investigative work make it difficult to schedule stories exactly, the editors aim to have one—perhaps even two—such major articles in each monthly issue.

For 1983, the Foundation budget allotted only about $30,000 to the investigative-journalism program.[123] Of course, this figure does not take into account the time regular staff members spend editing and publicizing the stories, nor does it reflect the publishing costs of the magazine itself. But however it is measured, the budget is extremely modest. *Reason* relies on the availability of interested writers who—for ideological or economic reasons—can be convinced to undertake a major project without much remuneration. Still, the editors take special pride in the investigative work, and apparently—if reader surveys can be trusted—*Reason* readers find those articles the most rewarding feature of the magazine.[124]

Reason is a slick, colorful magazine, and the publishers obviously work to make each month's cover visually arresting. But if the graphic design is aimed at stimulating newsstand sales, it has not been successful to date; only a small percentage of *Reason's* readers buy the magazine from local distributors.[125] In fact, the total circulation of the magazine is only about one-sixth that of *Mother Jones*: In 1982, it was still short of 30,000, but had climbed to almost 33,000 in 1983.[126] Nevertheless, those figures represent a substantial increase from earlier circulation counts, and both advertising sales and newsstand orders are said to be on the rise.[127] So it is possible that *Reason* might break into the ranks of the larger-circulation journals of political opinion in the future.

Even before that happens, *Reason* contributors can expect to receive a good deal of attention for their investigative work. Each featured article is advertised in press releases sent out to a list of newspaper editorial writers, television newsmen, and radio talk-show hosts. Within the last two years, *Reason* articles have led to stories on CBS' *60 Minutes*, ABC's *Nightline*, and *NBC Magazine*; articles have provided the grist for reports in *Newsweek*, the *Los Angeles Times*, *Wall Street Journal*, *Business Week*, *Chicago Tribune*, *Fortune*, and dozens of newspapers nationwide.[128] And the scope of the attention is not only national. The U.S. Information Agency has reprinted several *Reason* articles abroad, and translations have appeared in Sweden, Brazil, and Norway.[129]

Virtually all of the investigative pieces carried by *Reason* can be classified readily as either attacks on government expenditures or descriptions of more efficient private methods of replacing government services. Among the articles that have generated the most publicity have been: a report on NASA attempts to overrule Congressional authority;[130] an expose on fraud in weapons testing;[131] a report on how the State of Maine shut down its most effective prison program;[132] a critical analysis of the World Health Organization's study on infant formula;[133] and a graphic account of the dissipation of New York's subway system.[134] But not all the news is bad. *Reason* authors have also drawn attention to the successful efforts of neighborhood renewal movements in St. Louis,[135] and beneficial competition between electric utilities.[136]

Nor is *Reason* dedicated exclusively to the battle between the government and the private sector. At times, investigations have probed the workings of private organizations, such as Cesar Chavez's United Farm Workers and Tom Hayden's Campaign for Economic Democracy.[137] And at times the reporters have criticized government and private organizations alike. Perhaps the most dramatic of all *Reason* articles was a devastating indictment of government and media alike for their handling of reports that the Love Canal had been contaminated by chemical wastes.[138]

If the Reason Foundation literature is accurate, the magazine's investigative articles generate not only attention, but concrete results. There have been two national magazine awards—the John Hancock Award and the *Washington Monthly* Journalism Award.[139] The Foundation's annual report for 1981-82 claims that "six of the articles have led to legal decisions or legislative actions (including the cancellation of a NASA boondoggle and the introduction of legislation to reform military testing)."[140] Donald Hovde, then Undersecretary of Housing and Urban Development, called an agency staff meeting to discuss a *Reason* article.[141] And (according to the Foundation report), a high official in the Department of the Interior owes his position at least in part to the attention generated by his contribution to *Reason*.[142]

By any objective standard—size, circulation, advertising revenue, length of publication, or newsstand sales—*Mother Jones* dwarfs *Reason*. But if the measure of editorial efficiency is the attention an article attracts, or the results it produces, *Reason* has no reason to fear comparison with *Mother Jones*. To be sure, the parent Foundation puts its aggressive public-relations machinery behind each issue of the magazine; but presumably the Foundation for National Progress is equally determined to bring attention to *Mother Jones*. The comparative success of *Reason* is a tribute to the magazine's staff, and at the same time an intriguing demonstration of a very different style of investigative journalism.

Chapter I—Notes

1. Better Government Association publicity brochure (undated).
2. Michael Ver Meulen, "The Corruption Busters," *Quest*, June 1980, p. 64. See also Better Government Association annual reports.
3. The controversy was most dramatically covered by CBS' *60 Minutes* in a segment aired on April 24, 1983. See also the record of hearings held that month by the Permanent Investigations Subcommittee of the U.S. Senate Governmental Affairs Committee.
4. Ver Meulen, p. 61-62. See also Better Government Association 1977 Annual Report, pp. 2-11.
5. Ver Meulen, p. 100.
6. Better Government Association 1980 Annual Report, p. 43.
7. Author's conversation with BGA staff.
8. Ver Meulen, p. 100.
9. *Ibid.*
10. Better Government Association publicity brochure (undated).
11. *Ibid.* See also Better Government Association 1980 Annual Report, pp. 2-8. The ABC story aired in February 1980.
12. Rael Jean Isaac, *The Coercive Utopians* (Chicago:Regnery Gateway, 1983), p. 259.
13. Fund for Investigative Journalism publicity brochure (undated).
14. *Ibid.*
15. *Ibid.*
16. Fund for Investigative Journalism List of Grants and Books, 1980.
17. Seymour Hersch, *Cover-Up* (New York:Random House, 1972). This and the following two books were cited in the FIJ List of Grants and Books, 1980.
18. Jessica Mitford, *Cruel and Usual Punishment*, (New York:Fawcett, 1977).
19. Victor Marchetti and John D. Marks, *The CIA and the Cult of Intelligence*, (New York:Free Press, 1972).
20. FIJ letterhead and various printed materials.
21. *Ibid.*
22. Fund for Investigative Journalism brochures consistently call for material that is "factual as distinguished from ideological or philosophical."

23. FIJ materials cite a 1976 grant to Miles Copeland—a frequent contributor to *National Review*—for a story on U.S. corporate bribes in foreign countries. Actually, no article on that topic ever appeared in *National Review* under Copeland's byline.
24. David Armstrong, "A Thinking Approach to the News," *Columbia Journalism Review*, September/October 1978, p. 62.
25. *Ibid*, p. 61.
26. *Ibid*, p. 62.
27. *Ibid*.
28. *Ibid*.
29. *Ibid*.
30. Mary Jean Haley, "A Fresh Approach to Canned News," *New West*, January 30, 1978, p. 22.
31. Armstrong, p. 61.
32. From the Bay Area Institute's tax return, IRS Form 990.
33. Armstrong, p. 64.
34. Telephone interview with executive editor Jim Cooney, August 4, 1983.
35. Pacific News Service publicity brochure (undated).
36. Author's interview, April 1983.
37. Armstrong, p. 62.
38. Pacific News Service publicity brochure (undated).
39. Register and Tribune publicity brochure (undated).
40. Haley, p. 22.
41. Armstrong, p. 62.
42. Pacific News Service publicity brochure (undated).
43. PNS "Writer's Guide;" Form 990.
44. Form 990.
45. Articles of incorporation, filed with California Secretary of State.
46. *Mother Jones*, August 1978, p. 11.
47. Mark Dowie and Tracy Johnston, "A Case of Corporate Malpractice," *Mother Jones*, May 1977.
48. Figure cited in "Mother Jones Wins Tax Exemption Feud," *News Media and the Law*, January/February 1984, p. 47.
49. The *New Republic* reported a circulation as of December 1983 of 95,000. The *National Review* reported a circulation as of December 1983 of 96,600. From phone conversations with the magazines' circulation staffs.
50. Deirdre English, "Backstage," *Mother Jones*, May 1982, p. 5.
51. Center for Investigative Reporting brochure, "California Center Offers Educational Service," by Daniel Noyes.
52. David Weir, "Backstage," *Mother Jones*, July 1977, p. 5.
53. Mary Ann Hogan, "No Secrets," *Oakland Tribune*, July 15, 1981, p. E-1.
54. *Ibid*.
55. *Information Digest*, September 4, 1981, p. 244.
56. *Ibid*.

57. David Weir, Mark Schapiro, and Terry Jacobs, "The Boomerang Crime," *Mother Jones*, November 1979.
58. Hogan, "No Secrets."
59. *Information Digest*, p. 244.
60. Terry Pristin, "Cut-Rate News," *Columbia Journalism Review*, May/ June 1981, p. 42.
61. *Ibid*.
62. *Investigative Reports 1980-1981*, a clipping book provided by the CIR. In 1978 and 1979, the CIR had published an entire book to hold the year's stories.
63. *Ibid*.
64. *Ibid*.
65. Frank Prial, "Coast Freelance Unit Thrives on Reporting for TV," *New York Times*, September 10, 1983.
66. Hogan, "No Secrets."
67. *Investigative Reports 1978;-1979;-1980-1981*.
68. *Ibid*.
69. *Ibid*.
70. David Weir and Mark Schapiro, *Circle of Poison* (San Francisco: Institute for Food and Development Policy, 1981).
71. David Kaplan, "Where the Bombs Are," *New West*, April 1981, pp. 77-85.
72. CIR publicity brochure (undated).
73. Paradoxically, however, the Center for Investigative Reporting does not feel compelled to inform the citizenry—or at least certain citizens— about its own operations.

Old reports from the CIR listed an address in Oakland, California. So on a trip to the Bay area, I dialed their offices, and learned that the number had been changed. No problem; I dialed again. Explaining that I was working on a book commissioned by The Media Institute, I asked when I might visit to learn something about the Center's activities. The response was blunt; they would not see me. Well, could I come to their offices and collect some of their public literature? No. They would send the literature to me—at my home address across the country. The person to whom I spoke did not identify herself.

I could not drop the topic after such a conversation. Later in the day, I visited the Oakland address listed on the Center's material. No luck; the offices had been moved, and no one at the old address could give accurate directions. So I picked up the nearest telephone, and, reaching my old nemesis, asked for the address. But no, I was told; I would not need to visit. The literature would be sent to me. Later still, I made one more call, and another voice answered. The man blurted out the address, and then suddenly stopped in mid-zipcode. "Who is calling?" he demanded.

Eventually their "literature" did arrive—a single small pamphlet containing five paragraphs of information about the Center. But that pamphlet also mentioned that the Center offers four substantial books for sale to the public—books that (almost) anyone can buy simply by dropping in on their offices.

It struck me as curious indeed that an organization committed to investigative reporting—to bringing powerful private organizations under public scrutiny—would refuse so adamantly to cooperate with an inquiry into its own affairs.

74. Investigative Resources Center Annual Report, April 1, 1979-March 31, 1980, p. 12.
75. Author's observation during a visit to the IRC's offices.
76. ISLA publicity brochure (undated).
77. *Ibid.*
78. Data Center publicity brochure (undated).
79. IRC Annual Report 1979-1980, p. 4.
80. Data Center publicity brochure (undated).
81. Interview with staff, April 1983.
82. IRC Annual Report 1979-1980, p. 4.
83. IRC publicity brochure, "Corporate Profiles".
84. *Ibid.*
85. IRC publicity brochure.
86. *Ibid.*
87. *Ibid.*
88. IRC publicity brochure, "Resources for Understanding, Combatting, and Surviving the New Right."
89. *The New Right: Issues and Analyses*, Data Center Press Profile #5, and *The New Right: Fundamentalists and Financiers*, Data Center Press Profile #4.
90. *The New Right: Readings and Commentary*, the Data Center. See also the periodic *New Right Monitor Updates.*
91. *The New Right: Issues and Analyses*, Fall 1981, preface.
92. *Ibid.*
93. *New Right Monitor Update*, May 1982; and *New Right Monitor Update*, September 1982.
94. IRC Annual Report 1979-1980, p. 6.
95. *Ibid.*
96. IRC publicity brochure.
97. IRC Annual Report 1979-1980, p. 12.
98. *Ibid.*
99. Interview with FONR executive director Clarice Pool, April 1983.
100. The FONR provided the author of this book with an unpublished list of projects and grants.
101. Interview with Clarice Pool, April 1983.
102. Unpublished list at 100.
103. *Ibid.*

104. James C. Roberts, *Missing in Action* (Washington, Fund for Objective News Reporting, 1980).
105. FONR listing.
106. Tom Winter and Allan Ryskind.
107. John Chamberlain and M. Stanton Evans.
108. Interview with Clarice Pool, April 14, 1983.
109. Sabre Journalism Fund prospectus, p. 39.
110. *Ibid*, p. 3.
111. *Ibid*, p. 4.
112. *Ibid*, p. 5.
113. *Ibid*, p. 9.
114. Sabre Foundation prospectus.
115. Sabre Journalism Fund prospectus, pp. 13-38.
116. *Ibid*, p. 8.
117. *Ibid*, p. 10.
118. Telephone interview with Mark Frazier, May 16, 1983.
119. *Ibid*.
120. Reason Foundation Annual Report, Fiscal Year 1981-1982, p. 18.
121. *Ibid*, p. 8.
122. *Ibid*, inside front cover.
123. Telephone interview with Robert Poole, August 16, 1983.
124. *Reason Magazine Demographic Survey*, forthcoming from The Reason Foundation.
125. Telephone interview with Robert Poole, August 16, 1983.
126. 1982 circulation of 28,200 and 1983 circulation of 32,900. Cited by *Reason* circulation staff.
127. Annual Report 1981-1982, pp. 3-4.
128. *Newsworthy: The Reason Foundation Makes News*, The Reason Foundation, 1982. See also The Reason Foundation Annual Report, Fiscal Year 1981-82.
129. Annual Report 1981-1982, pp. 3-4.
130. *Ibid*, pp. 3-6.
131. *Ibid*.
132. *Ibid*.
133. *Ibid*.
134. *Ibid*.
135. *Ibid*.
136. *Ibid*.
137. *Ibid*.
138. Eric Zuesse, "Love Canal: The Truth Seeps Out," *Reason*, February 1981.
139. Annual Report 1981-1982, p. 3.
140. *Ibid*, p. 5.
141. *Ibid*, p. 4.
142. *Ibid*.

Chapter II: The Fine Art of Muckraking

What *is* investigative journalism? No one can write a newspaper column without basing it on facts, and to find facts one must do research. But the research involved in preparing an editorial column for a typical daily newspaper would not satisfy any definition of "investigation." When does editorializing end, and reporting begin? What distinguishes ordinary daily-newspaper reporting from special investigative work?

At times the distinctions might be blurred. Some stories in every daily newspaper come only after a great deal of reportorial legwork. The classic "scoop" is the product of investigative journalism: a story that comes to light only because one reporter has been especially diligent, or lucky, in following his leads. But the staple ingredient in every daily newspaper is something other than investigative reporting. On most days, in most cities, competing newspapers feature the same headline stories. To be sure, they might attach different levels of importance to those stories, their stories might include different facts, and the flavor of the writing might be quite different from one paper to the next. Still, the stories that constitute "hard" news do not vary from one editorial perspective to the next. An election, or a natural disaster, or a dramatic press statement by an embattled public official—such stories merit headlines in any respectable newspaper, and

35

if a town has more than one such journal, the same stories will appear on the front pages of each competing publication.

Beyond a common, consensual understanding of what constitutes the most important daily news, the mass media are also united by a similar approach to the process of gathering news on a day-by-day, week-by-week basis. Editors rely on regular information from the wire services; stories written or initiated by the Associated Press and United Press International account for hundreds of column-inches every day, and spark innumerable television and radio news items. Business reporters lean heavily on Dow Jones, so that each day, countless stories across the nation are based on the same announcement from Wall Street.

Outside the world of the stock market, reporters perform their daily duties with the help of a system less specific than the daily Dow Jones quotation, but no less authoritative. If they are not derived from the wire services, most stories are the products of either a press release or a press conference. Skillful public figures learn to use their press conferences carefully, so that in effect they write their own version of the next day's newspaper accounts. Effective public-relations experts develop the technique of writing press releases in journalistic style, so that reporters can write their stories simply by consulting the release. An experienced public speaker knows in advance which quotations the media will use in their coverage, and a talented publicist can choose the phrases that will be transferred intact from the press release onto the front page. To survive in politics, officials must learn to use, and manipulate, the media.

When a key public figure calls a press conference, dozens of reporters flock to the scene. When it is over, they head back to office telephones, and call on other people for comments that might fit into the same story. Often the circle of people who might be asked to comment is very small. When a political leader makes a statement, every reporter wants a comment from the leader of the opposition; when a union leader announces a strike, reporters quickly dial the corporate headquarters for its reaction. When events are developing quickly enough, one press release is answered immediately by another, and public officials match their rivals' press conferences in an effort to have the last word.

Prudent editors worry about all these efforts to manipulate their reporters. On the other hand, they have reason to rejoice as well; much of their work is done for them. If a reporter is particularly lazy, he might survive for a while merely by rewriting press releases. After all (he could reason), the relevant facts are already contained in the release. But conscientious journalists take the opposite tack. Realizing that every press statement carries a single biased perspective, ambitious reporters check the facts independently, and explore the private motives and suppressed facts that lie beneath every public statement. Then investigative journalism begins.

Every reporter must do his homework, whether or not investigative reports are his specialty. He must plow through dozens of press releases and wire-service stories, both old and new, that bear on the subject he is addressing. Then he must read other accounts of the same story, to see whether another reporter has discerned a special angle of approach. He must interview sources, attend public events, and take part in press conferences. All these activities form the base on which all reporting is built.

Investigative reporting opens a new dimension of reporting, above and beyond traditional journalistic techniques. With a particular subject in mind, the investigator begins by seeking out whatever public records might exist on his topic. If he is investigating an individual, the local registry of deeds should provide records of that individual's property and tax bills, and possibly records of his birth, marriage, and/or divorce. If the subject has been a party to any lawsuits, or been arrested on criminal charges, that information will also be available to the public.

Corporations, too, leave a trail of public documents. If the corporation offers stock for public sale, the Securities and Exchange Commission will have a cache of information concerning its affairs. Papers of incorporation can be obtained readily from the state in which the firm is registered. Corporations regularly file a document, called a "10-K," full of information about their contracts, management, salaries, and activities, with the Securities and Exchange Commission. Nonprofit organizations are required to provide similar reports ("Form 990") to the Internal Revenue Service. With a little work, and minimal expenses for copying, a reporter can have access to all these documents. Other government records can be obtained with a bit more effort, under the provisions of the Freedom of Information Act.

Case by case, a clever investigative reporter can discover more and more records to shed light on a subject. Some of these records are public documents. Others are private documents, but might be given freely to anyone who asks. Still others *should* be kept confidential, but a persistent reporter might convince the recordkeeper to let his defenses down. *Raising Hell*, a CIR guide to the techniques of investigative reporting, advises readers: "Probably the simplest rule to remember in requesting any record is to know as precisely as possible what it is you want and where, and then proceed as though you deserve it."[1]

Once all the available records have been obtained and digested, the reporter can turn to new sources. Invariably, those public documents will have sparked some leads: an old lawsuit might help to identify someone who has run afoul of the subject before, and has special information; a corporate contract might lead the investigator to explore another firm with which the original subject did business. Always, there is the financial trail: the record of how money changed hands, whence it came, and where it finally stays. Then there will be interviews, and confrontations, and more interviews, until the investigation reaches its objective.

The Better Government Association uses all of these techniques, and more. For a story on fraud in abortion clinics, some BGA staffers took receptionists' jobs at those clinics, while others came to the clinics carrying concealed cameras and asking for pregnancy tests. When some Chicago physicians were accused of performing unnecessary surgery, healthy BGA personnel visited those doctors—and were advised to undergo operations. To confirm their suspicions that a defense contractor was overcharging the Navy for mechanical parts, the BGA called the supplier and put in an order of its own. And in the famous "Mirage" caper, BGA staff actually owned and operated a tavern to expose corruption among building inspectors.

The Mirage investigation, which *Quest* magazine accurately described as "one of the most thorough and imaginative investigations into civic corruption ever mounted,"[2] uncovers several intriguing questions about investigative journalism. The miscreants were caught red-handed, with evidence provided by cameras, tape recorders, and marked bills. But to bring the hoax off successfully, the BGA had to take certain liberties. The Mirage tavern violated dozens of local ordinances; if it had been clean, city officials would have had no cause to suggest bribery. By its own admission, the BGA kept six different sets of fraudulent books for the tavern, to maintain appearances.[3] (A seventh, honest set of accounts kept the BGA safely on this side of the law.) BGA staff workers were carefully trained to avoid entrapment, so that indictments would stand up in court. All these measures took the BGA far afield from the journalist's standard investigation. The investigation was spectacularly successful. But was it journalism? One reply came from the Pulitzer Prize committee. The *Sun-Times*, which had cooperated with the BGA in the Mirage investigation, won a Pulitzer nomination for its story. But the committee had doubts about the propriety of undercover work by journalists, and the prize was awarded elsewhere.

For the BGA, the question of journalistic ethics was not directly relevant. The BGA is not a journalistic institution, strictly speaking. Rather, it concentrates on its investigations, and teams up with newspaper or television reporters to guarantee adequate coverage. The BGA technique is arduous, and involves heavy costs in time and money—especially when some investigations will turn nothing of any consequence. But the BGA is blessed with the time, money, and talent to continue in the same vein. Projects are selected carefully, to avoid unnecessary risk of failure; dramatic efforts come only when a preliminary search has indicated something amiss. Above all, the BGA avoids partisan political posturing. Unlike other investigative organizations, the BGA does not allow itself the luxury of interpreting its own findings. Since it relies on the media to provide accounts of its investigations, any political message would be subject to the mercies of outside reporters. Or, more likely, partisan reports would be treated like so much editorial gruel. To preserve its place in the world of journalism, the BGA must produce hard, reliable facts—facts that tell the story by themselves.

If the BGA harbors one persistent bias, it is an implicit belief in the ability of our political system to eliminate all corruption and inefficiency through a process of careful legal reform. Encountering waste, fraud, or incompetence, the BGA generally concludes that laws must be rewritten, or additional regulations devised; it seldom considers the possibility that a few dishonest individuals must have foiled a workable system. For example, when a BGA study of the Federal Railroad Administration showed that FRA inspectors regularly approved tracks that violated basic safety standards, the BGA hastened to conclude that the FRA needed fundamental reform.[4] Perhaps so; but could the problem have been solved even more expeditiously by firing the negligent inspectors? At times, the BGA approach suggests that all failures are institutional rather than individual—that a better-regulated world could eliminate the consequences of sloth, avarice, and incompetence.

In direct contrast with the BGA, the Pacific News Service thrives on interpretation rather than facts. Whereas the BGA is technically not a journalistic enterprise, PNS is not actually involved in investigations. As Alexandra Close puts it, the strength of PNS lies in its ability to provide "pathbreaking, innovative thinking."[5] The syndicate brings in experts from various specialized fields to take advantage of their expertise, but only rarely does it attempt to expose corruption after the fashion of classic muckrakers.

Ironically, a healthy portion of PNS' initial success can be attributed to its earlier work as a radical, investigative team. PNS beat the major outlets to the story of Korean CIA activities in the United States,[6] and that coup provided a major selling point when Close went out on her first nationwide promotional tour to attract subscribers. She described one incident to the *Columbia Journalism Review*:

> When I went to the *Washington Post*, I showed them our packet and Larry Stern, their national news editor, pointed out the Korean CIA story to [editor Ben] Bradlee. "Look, Ben," he said, "they had this eight months before we did."[7]

Viewed in retrospect, that accomplishment is less impressive than the account might suggest. The alternative press often beats established sources to news stories, since radical journalists often have access to radical political activists as informants. And until Close took the reins, PNS was undeniably aligned with the alternative press. Today, PNS is much more careful—careful to avoid the loss of credibility that would occur if a sensational story were disproven, and careful to camouflage the political biases of the syndicate.

But those political biases become clear to anyone who studies PNS material, or looks through the thumbnail descriptions of the PNS staff writers.[8] From the outset, PNS has been closely tied to the leftist Washington think tank, the Institute for Policy Studies (IPS). The list of PNS correspondents includes six men who have also served as IPS fellows: Richard Barnet (an IPS founder), John Dinges, Richard Falk, Michael Klare, James Ridgeway, and Franz Schurmann.[9] Among the other correspondents, radical political connections have been equally rife. Mansour Farhang was a senior foreign policy advisor to the Khomeini government in Iran. Nicole Szulc worked with Philip Agee, the former CIA agent who now specializes in exposing his former colleagues. And T. D. Allman responded to the imposition of martial law in Poland by writing that the event "may be remembered as the moment when Poland at long last freed itself of the suffocating oppression of the Polish Communist Party, and its petty bureaucrats..."[10]

To offset this preponderance of radical contributors, PNS has one regular correspondent, in a group of 34, who might be identified with conservative ideas: Robert Hawkins is director of the Sequoia Institute, an institution devoted to decentralizing government; he has served on advisory panels for the Reagan Administration.[11] In several lists of its published articles, PNS also proudly includes two other conservative writers: Denis Doyle of the American Enterprise Institute and Robert Wesson of the Hoover Institution.[12]

PNS has developed one peculiar stylistic device that furnishes a subtle vehicle for political ideology. In reports from foreign countries, PNS correspondents often view events through the eyes of a single person: a resident whose outlook on world events is, by implication, representative of the whole country's thoughts and concerns. Less frequently, but with equal effectiveness, PNS reports use the same technique to color American domestic politics, finding a suitable individual to represent the problems they mean to accentuate. The article, in either case, becomes a seductive cross between a human-interest story and an editorial statement. The reader, caught up in the life of an ordinary citizen like himself, does not stop to reflect on how carefully the correspondent must have selected his subject.

The technique is almost infinitely malleable. A PNS report from the Philippines criticizes the government indirectly by recounting the fears of a dissident clergyman.[13] To undermine the Pentagon's argument in favor of new nuclear weapons, a PNS feature takes the perspective of Moscow's military planners, and maintains that the Soviet arsenal is intended for use in defending Eastern Europe, while American missiles are poised to strike at the Russian homeland.[14] In each case, the PNS article amounts to an editorial column, wrapped neatly in the guise of a feature article.

The Center for Investigative Reporting lies midway on the continuum between the pure muckraking of the BGA and the masked editorializing of PNS. CIR stories do involve serious probes, and readers obtain plenty of information that they could not ordinarily find anywhere else. But CIR projects are guided by a consistent ideological pattern. The subjects of CIR investigations are usually corporate executives or government (especially military) officials. And the published stories that result are based on the underlying assumption that the machinations of corporate and military officers alike are inimical to the public weal.

In *Raising Hell*, a booklet published under the aegis of *Mother Jones*, CIR founder Dan Noyes explains the emphasis on probes into corporate affairs:

> A journalist once said that investigating business is a lot like sex: you get better with practice and it's not done enough....He might have added that business dominates our lives every bit as much as sex....Businesses and their owners have a vested interest in hiding as much information as they can, whether to protect themselves from competitors, avoid publicity or conduct illegal or extralegal activities for their own gain.[15]

If business is as dominant in our lives as sex, as Noyes thinks, then the commutative principle suggests that sex is as important as business. But the CIR never investigates sex. Putting the argument on a more serious level, the CIR never investigates the activities of "public-interest" law firms, or left-wing think tanks. Only once, among all the CIR stories published in the organization's annual collection, did a CIR reporter raise questions about the behavior of a liberal or radical activist; and even that story conveyed a striking message.

In a 1978 article published by *New Times* magazine, CIR grantees Kate Coleman and Paul Avery gave a harrowing, detailed description of how Huey Newton uses the remains of the Black Panther Party.[16] The article depicts a series of rapes, beatings, robberies, drug deals, intimidation of witnesses, and contract murders, all apparently masterminded by Newton, the leader of the Black Panther Party since its meteoric rise to prominence in the late 1960s. Many law-enforcement officials would contend that the story merely confirms the opinion they had always held of the Black Panthers. Then, remarkably, the tone of the CIR article changes:

> But, there is a growing sense among many sympathizers and ex-Panthers that it is Huey Newton himself who has discredited the Party—and, by seemingly gratuitous violence, betrayed the principles on which it was founded.[17]

Aside from the benign assumption that the original intentions of the Panthers were exclusively honorable, that paragraph betrays an attitude that, in investigative reporters, is exceedingly rare. When the

Better Government Association discovers corruption in a public institution, it calls immediately for reform; its recommendations proceed from the assumption that if an individual can wield unethical powers, the institution must share the blame. Instinctively, investigative reporters assume that instances of corruption are not isolated— that a single miscreant probably represents a whole class of peers whose offenses have escaped notice. Is it conceivable that a CIR story would uncover graft in a multinational corporation, and then imply that the illegal activities were the product of one misbegotten executive, soiling the reputation of an otherwise honorable firm? And yet, in their eagerness to uphold the Black Panther tradition, the CIR correspondents used just such logic.

Choosing their topics selectively, and viewing them through a specific ideological prism, CIR investigators are polemicists as well as muckrakers. They know the arguments they want to make, and take great pains to find corroborating evidence. Without exception, CIR products are well-written articles, and the authors demonstrate a firm grasp of the tools of rhetoric. CIR pieces, appearing as they do primarily in magazines with liberal or radical readerships, have the capacity to inflame an audience that shares the writers' prejudices, without actually proving any serious charge.

The publication of *Circle of Poison*[18] in book-length form, after an essay version won the National Magazine Award, constitutes the CIR's proudest achievement. In that book, and more particularly in the award-winning essay, David Weir and Mark Schapiro demonstrate that pesticides banned in this country are exported by their manufacturers for use in other countries—often the impoverished nations of the Third World. They go on to point out that foods raised in those countries are then imported for consumption by American citizens. All these facts appear irrefutable, and someone with an endemic suspicion of corporate affairs would find the story horrifying. From those established facts, a dedicated environmentalist could conclude that: American corporations are knowingly shipping poison to poor countries, and reaping a profit thereby; the U.S. government refuses to respond, presumably because corporate moguls control the regulatory agencies; and the food we import from those poisoned lands is now, gradually, killing us, too.

The arguments of *Circle of Poison* first appeared in *Mother Jones* and *The Nation*, where a readership dominated by radical activists and environmentalists probably did reach the conclusions listed above.[19] But imagine the readers' response if the same article had appeared in *Fortune* or *National Review*. Confronted with the very same facts, the new set of readers probably would have noted that: No one has ever conclusively demonstrated that most of the pesticides in question do in fact harm humans; without effective pesticides the natives of Third World countries would lose their crops to vermin, and starve; and the corporate leaders who engineer the deals are eating the same imported food as everyone else, so it seems unlikely that they are cavalier about the possibility of poison.

In another case, a CIR expose did involve some straightforward, apolitical muckraking to which *National Review* readers would respond in much the same fashion as the readers of *Mother Jones*. The story, in fact, appeared in *Mother Jones* in December 1978, and involved the "Hunger Project" and its connections with Werner Erhard's "est" program.[20] Author Suzanne Gordon, writing with typical CIR flair, pointed out that involvement in (and contributions to) the Hunger Project did nothing to solve the problem of world hunger; it simply attracted people (and money) into Erhard's "est" network. What the Hunger Project accomplished, Gordon declared, was not a cure for hunger but a feeling of irrelevant personal satisfaction. So far, so good. But no *Mother Jones* story could be complete without an ideological payoff. At the tag end of an otherwise impeccable presentation, the *Mother Jones* piece carried some suggestions for people who "really want to do something about famine and malnutrition." The sidebar suggested involvement with the Interfaith Center for Corporate Responsibility, the Institute for Food and Development Policy, World Hunger Year, or (for obscure reasons) the North American Congress on Latin America. All four organizations dwell in the radical camp; all "do something" about hunger by attacking American corporations. But one might be hard pressed to demonstrate how these groups actually spend their time and money feeding hungry people.

Since the Fund for Investigative Journalism does not actually produce written projects under its own steam, its political predilections are not so easily documented. But a survey of titles funded by the FIJ leaves little doubt that it, too, follows the logic of advocacy in investigation. The list is redolent of suspicions against the military, government intelligence, and corporations. Perhaps the simplest demonstration would be a listing of some of the books that have received FIJ subsidies:

- *Death in the Mines*[21]
- *CIA: The Myth and the Madness*[22]
- *Cover-up* (Seymour Hersch's expose on My Lai)[23]
- *Harvest of Death: Chemical Warfare in Vietnam and Cambodia* (published long before the Soviet Union was accused of chemical warfare there)[24]
- *The CIA and the Cult of Intelligence*[25]
- *The Vanishing Land: Corporate Theft of America's Soil*[26]
- *West Point—America's Power Fraternity*[27]
- *The Power Peddlers: How Lobbyists Mold U.S. Foreign Policy*[28]
- *Seizing Our Bodies*[29]
- *The American Way of Crime*[30]
- *Assassination on Embassy Row* (an account of the murder of Orlando Letelier)[31]

From the other side of the political debate, the Fund for Objective News Reporting could be charged, quite accurately, with the same sort of bias in its selection of worthy projects. Again, a mere listing of current FONR projects[32] tells the story adequately:

- Radio Moscow
- The Humanitarian Case Against the FDA
- American Intelligence Adrift
- Tom Hayden
- Suburban Guerillas
- The KGB
- The DGI (Cuban intelligence)
- The Institute for Policy Studies
- IRS *vs.* Independent Contractors
- Mail Lib: Repealing Private Express Statutes
- Billion Dollar Joke (the National Endowment for Humanities)
- Minimum Wage Law and Juvenile Crime
- Demystifying the Bureaucracy

Both *Reason* and *Mother Jones* nurture political ideals through editorial policies. In each case, the sponsoring organization—the Reason Foundation and the Foundation for National Progress, respectively—is a sort of "think tank" associated with a discernible political perspective. The Reason Foundation is most immediately concerned with pointing out the comparative virtues of the free market; the Foundation for National Progress specializes in questioning that economic system. So *Reason* editors look for those stories that will demonstrate the logic of their convictions: stories about the failures of government and/or the successes of private enterprise. *Mother Jones*, on the other hand, seeks out evidence of corporate rapacity and especially of crimes against the environment.

On rare occasions, the editors of *Reason* and *Mother Jones* might be equally interested in a given topic. (The *Reason* expose on Pentagon weapons testing[33] is probably a case in point; the story could have appeared in *Mother Jones* with no air of incongruity.) More often, the editors would probably react in a markedly different manner to an investigative reporter's proposal. A proposal to illustrate corporate tampering with environmental standards would pique the interest of *Mother Jones* editors, but excite no enthusiasm at the offices of *Reason*. Conversely, *Reason* would leap at the chance to show that a private firm had improved on government efforts to supply urban services; *Mother Jones* would find the story humdrum. In either case, the editors' selection of topics would probably be seconded by the magazine's readers. Depending upon their ideological presuppositions, different readers find interest in different topics, and different publications serve those predilections accurately.

Even the Investigative Resource Center, which compiles data to be molded into publishable form by others, shows its hand in the facts it collects most assiduously. In the crowded offices of the IRC Data Center, two huge boxes contain clippings about Ronald Reagan.[34] Naturally, an individual as prominent as the President generates a welter of newspaper comments. But the Reagan file dwarfs any other individual collection. Similarly, the Chase Manhattan Bank is covered by two substantial file boxes, while Bankers Trust—a financial institution of roughly equivalent size—merits only two slim folders.[35] Could IRC researchers be clipping only those pieces that arouse their own curiosity? Certainly the topics of the Data Center's "Press Profiles" betray an ideological bias. The Center has produced several volumes already analyzing the menace posed by conservative political activists;[36] there is no complementary probe of left-wing operatives. But, to their credit, IRC staff workers make no bones about the organization's ideological preferences.

Chapter II—Notes

1. Dan Noyes, *Raising Hell: A Citizens Guide to the Fine Art of Investigation* (San Francisco: *Mother Jones*, n.d.).
2. Michael VerMeulen, "The Corruption Busters," *Quest*, June 1980, p. 61.
3. Better Government Association 1977 Annual Report, p. 3.
4. Better Government Association 1980 Annual Report, pp. 9-11.
5. Mary Jean Haley, "A Fresh Approach to Canned News," *New West*, January 30, 1978, p. 22.
6. *Ibid*.
7. *Ibid*.
8. Pacific News Service publicity brochure (undated).
9. *Ibid*.
10. "Polandization: Keeping Warsaw in the Pact & Freedom in Warsaw," Pacific News Service, December 14, 1981.
11. Pacific News Service publicity brochure (undated).
12. *Ibid*.
13. William Christeson, "The Real Story Behind the People's Church," Pacific News Service, March 9, 1983.
14. Jon Stewart, "East, Not West, Is Target of Soviet Strategy," Pacific News Service, April 21, 1983.
15. Noyes, p. 11.
16. Kate Coleman and Paul Avery, "The Party's Over," *New Times*, July 10, 1978, pp. 11-27.
17. *Ibid*, p. 13.
18. David Weir and Mark Schapiro, *Circle of Poison* (San Francisco: Institute for Food and Development Policy, 1981).
19. David Weir, with Mark Schapiro and Terry Jacobs, "The Boomerang Crime," *Mother Jones*, November 1979; David Weir and Mark Schapiro, "The Circle of Poison," *The Nation*, November 15, 1980, p. 17.
20. Suzanne Gordon, "Let Them Eat est," *Mother Jones*, December 1978, pp. 45-63.
21. A. Britton Hume, *Death in the Mines* (New York: Grossman, 1971).
22. Patrick McGarvey, *CIA: The Myth and the Madness* (New York: Saturday Review Press, 1973).

23. Seymour Hersch, *Cover-Up* (New York: Random House, 1972).
24. E. W. Pfeiffer, *Harvest of Death: Chemical Warfare in Vietnam and Cambodia* (New York: Free Press, 1972).
25. Victor Marchetti and John D. Marks, *The CIA and the Cult of Intelligence* (New York: Knopf, 1974).
26. Frank Browning, *The Vanishing Land: Corporate Theft of America's Soil* (New York: Harper & Row, 1975).
27. Robert Johnson and Louis Frost, *West Point—America's Power Fraternity* (New York: Simon & Schuster, 1975).
28. Russell Howe and Sarah Trott, *The Power Peddlers: How Lobbyists Mold U.S. Foreign Policy* (New York: Doubleday, 1977).
29. Claudia Dreyfus, editor, *Seizing Our Bodies* (New York: Vintage Books, 1978).
30. Frank Browning and John Gerassi, *The American Way of Crime* (New York: Putnam, 1980).
31. Saul Landau and John Dinges, *Assassination on Embassy Row* (New York: Pantheon, 1980).
32. From a listing of current projects, Fund for Objective News Reporting, April 1983.
33. Dina Rasor, "Fighting with Failures," *Reason*, April 1982.
34. Author's observation during a visit to IRC offices.
35. *Ibid.*
36. *The New Right: Fundamentalists and Financiers*; *The New Right: Issues and Analyses*; *New Right Monitor Update, May 1982*; *New Right Monitor Update, September 1982*.

Chapter III: Reaching the Major Outlets

During the years of the Vietnam conflict, a host of underground newspapers began to appear in American cities, charging the U.S. government with all sorts of atrocities in its prosecution of the war. Most of the charges were unsubstantiated, and most have been proven insubstantial. But because the underground newspapers were ready to make such charges based on skimpy evidence, they did carry some accurate reports long before the other, established newspapers. When the "Pentagon Papers" first appeared in public print, those who read only the *New York Times* were shocked to hear suggestions that the U.S. government had conspired to oust President Diem. Anyone who read the underground papers regularly had first encountered that suggestion years earlier; it was one of the lesser charges aired by the alternative press. Yet the story was not taken seriously until the *Times* and the *Washington Post* printed it. Alternative journalism suffers constantly from this debilitating necessity: before a story is treated seriously, it must first appear in the nation's most prestigious newspapers, or on a major television network. In fact, political publicists lament that if you don't appear in the media, you don't exist.

According to their political preferences, some readers take stories on faith, not waiting for the major-media stamp of approval. A conservative author, writing for a conservative paper like *Human*

Events, can rest comfortably in the knowledge that his readers will credit his story even if the *New York Times* does not. (In fact, a true believer will find the suspicions of the *Times* as still more evidence that the story is accurate.) In like manner, a *Mother Jones* audience will accept indictments of big business as an article of faith, even when the national networks show their lack of conviction that the writer's theory holds water. *Reason* readers will not be inclined to look for special problems with a scheme to replace government social agencies with private entrepreneurs. So journalists can always reach an audience of their ideological confreres. The problem, of course, is that reaching such audiences is like preaching to the choir: it convinces no one who needs to be convinced.

Among the centers devoted to sponsoring investigative reporting, only the Better Government Association and the Fund for Investigative Journalism have succeeded consistently in reaching a market of major national outlets. The Center for Investigative Reporting has succeeded in this quest only by working closely with television investigative shows. The Reason Foundation has had both success and failure, each revealing in its own way. The Fund for Objective News Reporting has never, to date, managed to place an article in a publication outside its own ideological orbit.

The key to the BGA's success is the organization's credibility. Journalists know that the BGA has uncovered stories for a half-century, and its track record for verifiable reporting is excellent. When the BGA finds itself developing a strong head of steam in an investigation, and realizes that a story is in the making, the BGA staff calls on a media outlet—a television investigating team, or a local reporter, or even a wire-service correspondent—to join its investigative team as it pieces together the damning facts. Whatever their own convictions, journalists know that a phone call from the BGA presages a story worth pursuing. So the BGA finds a media outlet, the newspaper reporter (or television team) acquires an investigative story that seems promising, and both parties profit.

ABC's *20/20* program has been the BGA's most conspicuous television partner, but NBC has also cashed in on BGA leads: NBC's *Prime Time* and *News Magazine* shows have featured BGA material, as has *NBC Nightly News*. CBS' *60 Minutes* has also worked with the BGA.[1] Local affiliates of both ABC and NBC have used BGA reporting, but the CBS affiliate is conspicuously absent from this list. In fact, this affiliate produced a critical account of a BGA/ABC report on arson in Chicago.[2] BGA supporters claim the CBS affiliate was attempting to undermine the BGA's credibility; the CBS station retorts that the organization's investigative techniques were shoddy. Whatever the true reasons, the local CBS outlet and the BGA apparently have not yet found reason to cooperate.

Among newspapers, the Chicago *Sun-Times* has been the BGA's favorite partner, most memorably in the "Mirage" report.[3] But the *New York Times* has enjoyed a few BGA "scoops," and other beneficiaries have included UPI, the Cox Newspapers, the *Dallas Morning News*, *Washington Monthly*, *New Republic*, and others scattered around the country.[4] The *Chicago Tribune*, which won a Pulitzer Prize in 1971 for a BGA expose on private ambulance companies, apparently has not worked with the BGA recently.

Whether or not a BGA report first appears in one of the best-known media outlets, the most remarkable stories filter down to dozens of other publications. Who could resist re-telling a tale as sensational as the "Mirage" scam? Certainly not *Time* magazine, to mention only one.[5] When the BGA collects a convincing case against some public official or agency, and presents enough documentation to make the case readily understood, the appeal is overwhelming, and the number of outlets that use the material, in one form or another, is virtually unlimited. Unlike other organizations in the field, the BGA does not seem to make a concerted effort to keep track of all the columns sparked—directly or indirectly—by its work.

The successes of the Fund for Investigative Journalism take a very different form. Most FIJ projects result in magazine articles, or even in books, rather than in the sort of short, simple pieces that the mass media can readily digest. Quite a few FIJ projects have been adapted for use by major urban newspapers, but those adaptations appear as essays on newspaper op-ed pages, rather than as front-page reports. There have been exceptions; the *Washington Post*, *Baltimore Sun*, and *Boston Globe* have carried news features based on FIJ reporting.[6] But ordinarily the appeal of FIJ features is geographically limited. In 1978, when Richard Fineberg studied competition to build the Alaskan pipeline, the *Alaska Advocate* sought the story.[7] Jacqueline Sharkey's coverage of discrimination in South Tucson appeared in *El Independiente*,[8] a student-run paper at the University of Arizona. A 1980 look at New Mexico's prisons reached the *Albuquerque News*.[9] One noteworthy FIJ story, a charge of torture in Chile, was picked up by UPI after first appearing in the *Village Voice*.[10] But ordinarily the first fruits of FIJ projects appear in essay form, in magazines of persuasion rather than in news outlets.

The Center for Investigative Reporting, in its first years of operation, leaned heavily on *Mother Jones*; at times the connection was so tight that *Mother Jones* seemed to be the Center's publishing arm.[11] (Or, perhaps more accurately, the CIR seemed a subsidiary of *Mother Jones*—an appearance that is not too far from the truth.) Only after four years of operation did the CIR begin to place articles in apolitical magazines such as *California Living*;[12] even today those stories are exceptions.

However, when Lowell Bergman left the CIR to climb the hierarchy of the ABC news organization, the group he had helped to found discovered an exciting new possibility. In short order the CIR had become a regular adjunct of ABC's *20/20* team, and soon thereafter the organization became affiliated with CBS' *60 Minutes* as well.[13] In each case, the CIR's role in the television production process was to seek out likely stories, and to provide the preliminary research on which the television stories would be built. Mike Wallace of *60 Minutes* extolled the virtues of this arrangement to *TV Guide*, saying that CIR provided "eyes and ears for us out West."[14]

TV Guide, however, saw dangers in the way *60 Minutes* used the CIR and other outside agents:

> Still, the idea that *60 Minutes*, television's most admired model of journalistic independence, sometimes solicits outside sleuthing talent—well, it raises certain questions: Questions about why this outside help is needed. Questions about accuracy. Questions about fairness and balance.[15]

Of those three sets of questions, the first is readily answered. Andrew Hacker, writing in *Fortune*[16] even before the *TV Guide* article appeared, did some plain arithmetic about the way *60 Minutes* is prepared. To the viewer, the program presents only four faces each week; the same few correspondents cover every story. Since *60 Minutes* covers subjects spanning locations all over the world, and since each story involves countless hours of digging for facts and waiting for interviews, it should be obvious, on a moment's reflection, that Mike Wallace and his on-air colleagues do not perform the full investigations by themselves. Quite the contrary. The *60 Minutes* team includes 32 producers, who receive only fleeting recognition in the program's credits. *60 Minutes* draws special benefits by relying on four familiar faces—correspondents the viewer feels he knows. As Hacker pointed out, "Were the show to employ, say, 32 different correspondents the dramatic effect would hardly be the same."[17]

In effect, however, *60 Minutes does* have 32 different correspondents. Each producer takes an investigative lead, develops the story, searches out the relevant parties, does the tedious legwork involved in providing factual evidence, and then turns the story over to the "star" correspondent and his camera crew. Like any other television program of similar size and scope, *60 Minutes* is utterly reliant on a large team of supporters to do the hard work before the cameras begin rolling.

If television producers were investigative reporters, the connection with groups like the CIR would be unnecessary. But television is a medium that demands constant action, and people who are attracted to a career in the field are rarely gifted with the patience that painstaking research requires. The ABC decision to hire Lowell Bergman, and then quickly promote him to head its investigative teams, reflects the network's realization that good investigators are hard to find. The fact that he was soon enticed over to CBS, to work as a producer for *60 Minutes*, reinforces the point. Bergman himself confirmed that problem in a 1981 conversation with the *Columbia Journalism Review*. No doubt frustrated by the practices of his new colleagues, he lamented that "most television news producers can't find their way around a county recorder's office."[18]

Moreover, the sheer volume of reporting necessary to sustain a program like *60 Minutes* calls for a great deal of cooperation from outside organizations. Members of the CBS production staff who seek out leads for *60 Minutes* stories rely on dozens of individuals and organizations already familiar with the topic, leaning heavily on the information they glean from their first interviews with people active in the field. If the story sounds promising, the *60 Minutes* team will take charge, checking facts and conducting interviews independently. But without that first boost—to help distinguish between worthwhile stories and false leads—they could never do all the work by themselves.

Who provides that initial guidance? Sometimes the television producers can rely on public officials, or others who are directly involved in the issue under discussion. At other times, however, the help will come from people who have already done some preliminary research—occasionally even from people who have developed the story completely on their own. Usually that assistance comes through long, exhaustive interviews, and through invitations to browse through existing files. Rarely will television programs actually pay for the investigative work that develops a useful story. Still more rarely will producers keep investigators on retainer, trusting that their steady production will justify the costs.

Television investigative teams need help from outside. What sort of help? Bergman again provided the answer, this time for *TV Guide*: "Any reporter—Establishment or otherwise—pursues the issues that he or she is interested in. Somebody once said that investigative reporting requires a certain degree of outrage, and I believe that."[19]

So television requires two things to make its investigations successful. The networks must enlist the help of people who have both expertise and a sense of outrage—the ability to plumb the secrets of a county recorder's office, and the ideological fervor to pursue their chosen prey relentlessly. Still, the networks would not count on reporters whose work did not match their specifications. Perhaps ABC and CBS do not have the special investigative talents of the CIR, and perhaps their correspondents do not feel the outrage that fuels the investigator's ardor. But neither *20/20* nor *60 Minutes* would use CIR stories unless they enjoyed the results.

Both *20/20* and *60 Minutes* have worked with the BGA as well as the CIR.[20] But a crucial distinction between the two organizations should be made. BGA stories appear not only on these television news programs, but also in newspapers and magazines of varying ideological stripe all around the country. If a CIR idea cannot be translated into a television expose, it is probably fated to appear in *Mother Jones*. Neither CBS nor ABC has worked with the Fund for Objective News Reporting or the Sabre Foundation to find investigative reporters whose sense of outrage reflects a conservative disposition.

When *TV Guide* assayed CIR and its relationship to the network news magazines, the major focus of the story was on the question of journalistic ethics. But ironically, that story concentrated on relatively minor problems, while missing the most obvious questions about professional propriety. To be sure, the *TV Guide* story demonstrated that not all *60 Minutes* stories derive exclusively from the work of the CBS *60 Minutes* team. But surely that news is neither surprising nor alarming. Anyone who understands the needs of the network producers should also understand the need for outside help. But from that point, the next logical step would be to question why the networks choose the CIR to provide that help. And that is the question *TV Guide* never asked.

Instead, the *TV Guide* story took another intriguing tack, and asked why the networks were not more forthright in admitting their reliance on outsiders. Geraldo Rivera of ABC's *20/20* answered that question comfortably enough: "I write their names into the script when we use them; we show them on camera, and I mention them every third or fourth paragraph."[21] But Mike Wallace of *60 Minutes* expressed a much more cavalier attitude: "Look, we all, to a greater or lesser extent, live off one another in this business."[22] He saw no reason to change the *60 Minutes* practice of naming outside helpers only in the credits at the end of the show.

Although Wallace made the point crudely, he came a bit closer to the crux of the ethical puzzle. The treatment that investigative reporters receive at the hands of the major networks is, after all, a private affair. If the CIR had objected to the scanty credit it earned on *60 Minutes*, it would not have continued working with CBS. Clearly, the CIR and *60 Minutes* had decided to "live off one another." But why? Why did CBS choose to "live off" the CIR, and why did the CIR accept such treatment at the hands of CBS?

Two years after that article appeared in *TV Guide*, media critics were still asking the wrong questions, ignoring several obvious clues. In September 1983, the *New York Times* reported that the CIR had developed a special contractual arrangement with KRON-TV, the NBC affiliate in San Francisco.[23] On this occasion, the story concentrated on the financial implications of the deal. *Times* reporter Frank Prial pointed to the most obvious reason why KRON would enjoy such an arrangement: "A network reporter with little or no experience in deep investigative work may earn $85,000 a year; *60 Minutes* correspondents may earn $500,000 or more. A CIR reporter...may earn $15,000."[24]

But Sy Perlman, of NBC's *First Camera* show, found a troubling aspect to the arrangement. By now, he noted, the CIR was working not only with KRON but also with *60 Minutes* and *20/20*. In short, the CIR had a foothold somewhere in each of the three largest national television networks. Commented Perlman, "My problem is, how does one go to a group already dealing with the other two networks? Who gets which story, the show with the best ratings?"[25]

The *Times* story (which, the author admits, was written at the suggestion of a friend on the CIR's board of directors[26]) pondered the financial arrangements that linked the CIR with so many different television outlets. Once again, the conclusion was interesting but not alarming. The CIR does, indeed, gain a financial advantage from its television contacts. But the figures are too small to warrant much attention; with a salary level still around $15,000 the CIR is not, by any stretch of the imagination, a road to riches.

Still, it is interesting that a small organization such as the CIR would have so many powerful outlets for its work. And it is downright fascinating that television producers would not balk at the prospect of sharing the CIR's work-product with their competitors. What gives the CIR such special appeal?

The relationships between television producers and the Reason Foundation lends another perspective to the story. On several occasions, network broadcasts have used material from *Reason* investigative stories. In 1981, ABC's *Nightline* featured the *Reason* analysis of the Love Canal affair; NBC picked up the investigation of the United Farm Workers, and CBS' *60 Minutes* reworked Dina Rasor's account of fraud in Pentagon weapons testing.[27] In each of these cases, however, the television story was broadcast *after* the story first appeared in the pages of *Reason*.

Like the BGA, the Reason Foundation has been able to interest television reporters in stories that are already thoroughly researched and developed. And in the case of *Reason*, the network has no need to contact the sponsoring organization; the author of the article can provide all the necessary information himself. (The same would hold true if the networks took an interest in research sponsored by the Sabre Foundation or the FONR; in each case, the research material would come from an independent investigator, not from the organization.) The research is already done; the story is already developed and perhaps even printed. Using that complete set of materials as a jumping-off point, the television producers can easily adapt the story to their own medium.

When someone else has already provided the foundation, the networks do not, ordinarily, need to offer much financial incentive to induce cooperation. Someone whose research has already produced a major magazine article is generally willing to answer a few follow-up questions, and to let the television reporters use his background notes and information. After all, what else can he do with that material? So when *Reason* authors or BGA personnel cooperate with *60 Minutes* or with *20/20*, they expect no financial rewards. Only on rare occasions, when the *remaining* research exceeds the abilities of the television investigative team, do the outside reporters win a contract. Ari Maravel, press spokesman for *60 Minutes*, could recall only two instances of such contract work in recent months: CBS paid Dina Rasor for work on the weapons-testing story, and, of course, the CIR is regularly paid for its investigative work on the West Coast.[28]

The success of the CIR, then, is unique in two different ways. First, the CIR is paid as an institution. The networks do not make arrangements with individual reporters, but enlist the full resources of the journalistic cooperative. Second, the CIR is paid to do *preliminary* research: to develop stories rather than to hand over the products of completed investigations. Lowell Bergman recalls that, while at ABC, he drew up a contract with his old CIR colleagues that gave ABC a "right of first refusal" on new CIR stories.[29] The BGA or Reason Foundation might give *60 Minutes* some tips for a story, but that story would become public with or without *60 Minutes*. But the CIR not only does research, but actually develops ideas for new investigations. In effect, the CIR suggests stories, and the networks follow up.

Under any ordinary circumstances, network shows would assiduously avoid situations in which outsiders might determine—or even *seem* to determine—what stories should be broadcast. But in their relationships with the CIR, the major networks place themselves in exactly that situation. By taking the product of CIR investigations as the basis for their stories, they accept the CIR's choice of appropriate subject matter.

Or, to put the matter in a different light, the networks in effect subsidize whatever research the CIR plans to undertake. Left to their own devices, CIR reporters might not be able to muster the financial resources necessary for a full-scale investigation; a television retainer makes all the difference. Dan Noyes made the point abundantly clear when the *Columbia Journalism Review* asked why the CIR worked so closely with the networks. Referring to one prominent CIR success, a *20/20* segment on a 1950s nuclear test program called "Operation Wigwam," Noyes pointed out that "We never would have been able to do that investigation without ABC."[30]

Even if the CIR were purely a journalistic cooperative, with no sign of political bias, this symbiotic relationship with television would be questionable. But the CIR is not at all apolitical. Each CIR investigation bespeaks a certain discernible political outlook. And when the CIR staff produces its own work, without the intervention of television correspondents, the result has an unabashed political charge. An *Oakland Tribune* report on the CIR's "Circle of Poison" expose pointed out that the investigation had left straight news reportage far behind: "Schapiro and Weir have gone beyond the point of merely reporting the problem. They are concerned about the moral and health issues involved and they openly advocate change."[31]

Ordinarily, one would expect a chorus of reaction from media critics, questioning the propriety of the networks' open support for a group connected with political advocacy. But no such outcry has been heard. After researching the CIR for the *New York Times*, Frank Prial complained that he had trouble finding a criticism of the organization; none of the producers and editors he contacted voiced any complaints whatsoever about the CIR's work. Nor could Prial see a question of political bias. Rather, he thought, the CIR merely reported the stories that the networks wanted. As Prial put it, "They deal in a certain part of the media world where there is an acceptance of fundamentals."[32]

What would happen if a network worked cooperatively with a group unlike the CIR—a group outside the "certain part of the media world" that Prial describes? Would media critics remain silent if the outsiders' choice of subjects did not match the ordinary preferences of the network producers themselves? As it happens, a recent controversy involving *60 Minutes* provides the answer.

The story began when a *60 Minutes* staff member started doing preliminary work for a story on the political role of American churches. Early in that process, she approached Penn Kemble, the executive director of the Institute on Religion and Democracy (IRD), a Washington-based organization set up to counteract radical activism within American churches. As Kemble recalls it, the correspondent said she was looking for an interesting angle—something that would dramatize the churches' political involvement.[33] Kemble was delighted to oblige; his organization had compiled a formidable amount of information to demonstrate that the National Council of Churches was providing financial support for terrorist activities in several different countries. By inference, that revelation meant that ordinary American churchgoers, when they put their weekly offering on the collection plate, were helping the cause of violent revolution. The dramatic impact of that story was obvious, and within a few months

60 Minutes produced a special double-length story based on the IRD material.[34]

In the immediate aftermath of that *60 Minutes* episode, the National Council of Churches came under heavy criticism. But so did CBS and the IRD. Attempting to rebut the charges levelled against them in the *60 Minutes* episode, officials of the church group complained that the entire story had made CBS a vehicle for IRD propaganda.[35] In a certain sense, that was true. Anyone familiar with the IRD recognized the facts presented by *60 Minutes*; they had been discussed regularly in IRD literature. The IRD had provided *60 Minutes* with an idea, a set of evidence, and even the argument that would place all the pieces in the proper context.

In this, evidently, there was nothing unusual, save for the fact that the group supplying CBS with all this material was regarded as a conservative organization. Presumably the CIR has similar scope when its research appears on *60 Minutes*. In fact, the CIR has much greater scope. The IRD labored for months, developing the material that would eventually become the *60 Minutes* episode, before CBS happened to contact it. Like many other public-affairs organizations, the IRD had been longing for just such an opportunity to bring its message to a broad national audience. But the CIR has that same opportunity regularly. By virtue of their special relationship with the network producers, CIR investigators can be sure that many, if not most of their ideas will find a sympathetic audience.

Perhaps, if there were more conservative groups gathering facts as painstakingly and exhaustively as the IRD had gathered facts to indict the church-related charities, network producers would feature more conservative stories. What the television networks seek is a story idea that will be lively, revealing, and, if possible, shocking. Television is an entertainment medium, and the impact of a story can be measured by its ability to grip the audience. But in order to provide such gripping stories, one must first find hard evidence that something is seriously wrong with an American institution. The IRD story, showing the corruption of church bureaucracies, did just that. Typically, however, conservative groups *defend* established institutions. Still, there are some conservative groups that do indulge in muckraking among established institutions. Especially when the story line involves the waste of taxpayers' dollars, a host of investigative journalists stands ready to provide the hard facts—among them, those supported by the Fund for Objective News Reporting and the Sabre

Foundation. Such stories rarely appear on *60 Minutes* or similar programs. The IRD episode was a rare conservative venture in a field generally more sympathetic to liberal political views—a field in which, as Frank Prial put it, "there is an acceptance of fundamentals."[36]

And the IRD story was a particularly dramatic one. What could be more shocking than the charge that church contributions helped support political terrorism? That story was too good to miss. Indeed, *60 Minutes* took the unusual step of devoting two-thirds of a weekly program to the subject. And the resultant controversy confirms the producers' judgment that this was an especially controversial topic. In a word, the IRD had provided a story so compelling that *60 Minutes* could not pass it up. When the topic is less sensational—a mere case of government waste or incompetence—the networks are less inclined to hear conservative voices. In such cases, the edge goes to the CIR.

Here again, the experience of the Reason Foundation is instructive. True, *Reason* stories have been featured on each of the three networks.[37] But none of these stories involved tales of waste in government social programs—the most common subject of *Reason* investigations. Apparently the central focus of *Reason* editorial policy does not match the interests of television producers; *Reason's* editors and network producers do not "share fundamentals." The revelation of fraud in Pentagon tests appeals to *60 Minutes* in a way that the quashing of an effective prison rehabilitation program does not.

Evidently, the CIR staff elicits special attention from television's investigative journalists—for something more than their competence as investigators. Simply put, the stars of television journalism seem to approve of their objectives. When the CIR launches a campaign to expose some American institution, television producers assume that they, too, would like to see that institution exposed. Otherwise, why would they subsidize the CIR efforts? Could this explain the comments of Dave Marasch, a former *20/20* producer, who told the *Columbia Journalism Review* that CIR staffers were not only good journalists, but also "great and wonderful people"?[38]

Television producers and celebrity correspondents might not be ready to embark on the CIR's crusades—they might not feel the same sense of outrage that motivates the investigators—but they are happy to see the CIR prosper. The CIR furnishes ideas, *i.e.* finds villains for investigative pieces, and the networks signal their tacit approval. To borrow Mike Wallace's phrase, the "alternative" investigators and the best-known correspondents "live off one another"[39] ideologically as well as financially. In more ways than one, organizations like the CIR do the dirty work for establishment journalists.

Not that the CIR staff minds doing that sort of work. On the contrary. Despite the profits to be made in television journalism, the CIR finds itself losing money on some of its jobs for the networks. The CIR estimates that a typically intensive six-month investigation costs about $10,000.[40] Retainer fees from the two networks (excluding the local contract with KRON in San Francisco) amounted to only a few hundred dollars a month, plus a certain amount for each episode the networks use.[41] When the CIR's work first appeared on ABC's *20/20* in an expose of the "International Year of the Child," the cooperative was paid only $1,000.[42] The next joint venture with ABC, on "Operation Wigwam," netted $8,000, but involved six months of work by six CIR reporters.[43] After a few years of success, the CIR likely commands a higher price. Still, the work is not lucrative— particularly in comparison with the high-paying jobs of the television correspondents propped up by CIR material.

But keep in mind that CIR personnel are not overly concerned about making a profit. Their cooperative is nonprofit in every sense of that term, and they themselves are grossly underpaid by the standards of their profession.[44] The career of Lowell Bergman illustrates how quickly a CIR reporter can climb the career ladder in the major networks; the investigative expertise of a CIR reporter is badly needed in the "establishment" press. Yet, aside from Bergman himself, no CIR staff members have climbed that career ladder. CIR workers are rewarded not with money, nor with the blandishments of future career prospects, but with the personal gratification that comes from sending an ideological message to a broad national audience.

No doubt this attitude helps explain the symbiotic relationship between the CIR and its network sponsors. Each party is exploiting the other, each according to its own purpose. The networks are getting good investigative reporting at a cut-rate cost. The CIR is getting national exposure. But then, the attitude of the CIR is not unusual; many people will endure great sacrifices to have their work appear on national television. What is much more intriguing is the networks' apparent delight with the CIR.

The most influential journalists of the mass media adhere to a very distinct world-view; that fact has been demonstrated irrefutably. Poll after poll confirms that the people involved in the mass media are distinctly more liberal in their political and social attitudes than the mass of American society.[45] The people who have the greatest opportunity to shape American public opinion look upon the world with a set of attitudes very different from the attitudes of their audiences. In the world of television, this prevailing set of attitudes inclines producers toward a certain type of investigative story—the type that the CIR turns out so skillfully. Perhaps television producers do not nurture the same violent antipathy toward corporate America that leads the CIR to focus its probes on business firms. (Lowell Bergman's success, however, suggests that such antipathy is not foreign to the networks.) But those producers do at least share the CIR's mistrust for American business. The differences—assuming that there are differences—are of degree.

Television producers are not alone in this willingness to cooperate with radical activists. In the print media, the Pacific News Service has a track record as impressive as the CIR's record in broadcasting. About 175 newspapers around the country subscribe to PNS through the *Register and Tribune* syndicate,[46] and that number includes such well-known papers as the *Washington Post, Los Angeles Times, Philadelphia Inquirer, San Francisco Examiner, Boston Globe,* and *Chicago Tribune.* That success belies the statement of Dennis Allen, president of the *R & T* syndicate, that "PNS is a little gem—one of the best kept secrets in American journalism."[47]

The special appeal of PNS is similar to that of the CIR, but the print medium does make some crucial differences. For a small-town newspaper editor, PNS furnishes an economical means of providing diversity on the editorial page. Mike Cooper, editor of the Fairbault (Minnesota) *Daily News,* uses PNS copy regularly for his op-ed page. Cooper points out that PNS can furnish a variety of different authors, thereby avoiding the monotony that afflicts some small-paper editorial pages.[48] And PNS has no real competition in this field; no other syndicate provides a regular feed featuring different writers in every week's packages.

Still, Cooper does recognize a distinct perspective in the PNS material—a perspective strong enough to keep PNS confined to his op-ed pages. As he puts it, "I see them as having a bias. It's not exactly a political bias; it's more in their choice of topics."[49] Cooper passes up some PNS features that he thinks his readers would ignore; he suspects that the PNS perspective—by comparison with his readers' interests—is "more particularly concerned with the arms race and that sort of thing."[50] Peter Selkowe, editor of the *Southern Illinoisan*, sees the same ideological overtone, but welcomes it: "An editorial page is the place for opinion, after all, not just neutered ramblings."[51]

In considering PNS material as editorial copy rather than news analysis, Cooper and Selkowe stand squarely opposite Jim Cooney, the executive editor of the *R & T* syndicate, who looks upon the PNS product as "very objective."[52] On the other hand, their judgment matches that of another local newspaper editor, Harvey Myman of the *North East Bay Independent and Gazette* in Berkeley, California. "Within their stories," Myman told the *Columbia Journalism Review*, "they're very balanced and fair."[53] Still, "PNS's bias shows in their selection of stories."[54]

Ironically, it is precisely the selection of topics that seems to appeal to editors of other, larger papers. For a large urban newspaper, PNS diversity is not such an important consideration. But Tom Baxter, national editor of the *Atlanta Journal*, has another reason for favoring the syndicate: "It is grounded in a good sense of what subjects— crime, housing, and money, to name three—matter to the American newspaper reader."[55] Robert Maynard of the *Oakland Tribune* feels "the value of PNS to American journalism lies in its willingness to explore subjects more conventional media rarely approach."[56] The *Boston Globe's* Tim Leland enthuses: "PNS seems to be on the cutting edge of a lot of issues in ways I find quite usable."[57]

Small-town editors find PNS usable because it provides lively commentary. City editors, however, find it usable because PNS correspondents choose the "right" topics. That arrangement seems to duplicate the relationship between the CIR and the national news networks. Once again, the "alternative" reporters help their "establishment" colleagues primarily by choosing the proper topics, and taking the proper initiatives.

PNS is not alone in profiting from the ideological affinity that binds established print journalists with more radical ideological warriors. In 1977, when David Weir's "Circle of Poison" story won the National Magazine Award for *Mother Jones*, the magazine issued a special notice to its readers, reporting that "Indeed, it seemed as if the editors and writers from all the other magazines were pleased to celebrate our success."[58]

Leanita McClain, editor of the "Perspectives" section of the *Chi-*

cago Tribune, says it all in a quotation found in the PNS promotional brochure: "PNS tends to find the proper balance between liberal and conservative viewpoints and is always provocative."[59] The word "provocative" is crucial; large media outlets are commercial ventures, and their products must capture the audience's attention. Unlike their counterparts in the alternative press, mass media leaders cannot let their ideological preferences color their perception of how a story will be greeted by the marketplace. That, in a nutshell, is the difference between established and alternative press reporting.

But the woman responsible for the *Chicago Tribune's* editorials, from her perch in the mainstream of establishment journalism, acknowledges more than simply the provocative nature of PNS stories. She also reveals a deeper message, for she adds that PNS—a fosterchild of the Institute for Policy Studies, the nation's most active leftist institution with one token conservative among its 34 regular correspondents—"tends to find the proper balance between liberal and conservative viewpoints."[60] The "proper" balance, apparently, gives a mighty advantage to the activists of the political left. Thus runs the logic of the mass media.

Recall the dictum of Lowell Bergman: that investigative reporters need a "sense of outrage." In the perception of the alternative investigators, the product of investigation should convey that outrage, mobilizing the reader (ideally) into political activism of his own. CIR staffers David Weir and Mark Schapiro confess that their book *Circle of Poison* is intended to shock and outrage the reader. And *Circle of Poison*, it should be noted, won favorable reviews from papers and magazines all around the country. The Fourth Estate might not share the passions of CIR reporters, but it is ready to listen. Perhaps the CIR material seems extreme, but it is "usable."

The capacity to "shock and outrage"—or the lack of it—might explain one of Robert Poole's frustrations. The editor of *Reason* points out that while his magazine's exposes on government corruption and inefficiency are reasonably well received by the major media, newspaper and television reporters tend to ignore the other staple of *Reason's* investigative diet: stories illustrating the ability of the private sector to replace government social programs.[61] When a public servant is caught with his hand in the till, every editor immediately recognizes a story. But editors who are accustomed to seeking governmental solutions to social problems do not have the same quick, instinctive appreciation for a story about efficiency in the private marketplace.

Ironically, Poole reports that such stories *do* generate a good deal of interest among talk-show hosts.[62] Free from the demands of pursuing daily headlines, and avid for a new "angle" that will excite listeners, radio hosts are more than willing to explore radical new ideas. Is it too much to suggest that these radio hosts are sponsoring more genuine groundbreaking journalism than their sophisticated cousins in newspaper and television newscasting? Do seasoned "investigative" reporters miss some of the most interesting stories because their ideological preferences limit their vision?

Some of the most sophisticated investigative groups, notably the CIR and PNS, have learned to focus on topics that rank high on the liberal agenda without actually joining in the partisan political controversy. For example, both the CIR and PNS have paid special attention to the environment—an issue that fits beautifully into their political perception without being ostensibly partisan. Everyone wants a liveable world, and no one enjoys pollution; so a story describing the dangers of pollution may not ring the mental warning buzzers that tell readers an ideologically charged message is on the way. Nevertheless, by recounting tale after tale of corporate neglect for the environment, investigators convey their fundamental distrust for American business.

Those who applaud the activists can echo the words of Mike Cooper: "Often they're avant garde, warning of approaching national and international problems."[63] But the same point could be made in other words: the CIR and PNS have learned how to choose topics, which, despite their heavy ideological overtones, are not yet recognized as partisan issues.

Another key to the companion successes of the CIR and PNS is that each organization styles itself as an organ of the news media, rather than as an advocacy group. The Reason and Sabre Foundations, by contrast, are think tanks unabashedly promoting a point of view; so is the Foundation for National Progress, the publisher of *Mother Jones*. When any of these organizations releases information to the mass media, that information is naturally subject to special scrutiny. Newspaper and television reporters do not accept press releases from advocacy groups unquestioningly. A group that claims membership in the journalists' fraternity can pass inspection much more easily. In short, if an advocacy group makes a dramatic announcement, that constitutes a *lead* for a news story. If a news organization makes the same sort of announcement, that *is* the story.

If the situation is really quite so simple, then groups such as the

CIR and PNS should soon have competition. Ideologically based think tanks could spin off subsidiary news organizations to bridge the gap between advocacy and journalism. But to be successful, such hybrid groups would need sponsors as influential as *60 Minutes*, *20/20*, and the *Register and Tribune* syndicate. Preparing news stories, after all, is only half the battle; the other half is convincing the media to carry those stories. If the new, competing groups were perceived as ideologically biased, they would be forced to overcome that perception, or to find editors and producers who shared their bias.

To date, no competing groups have had much success in imitating the CIR and PNS. The conservative Heritage Foundation runs a syndicate offering newspaper feature stories, but those stories are carried on editorial and op-ed pages; they are not classified as news. No organization to the right of the political center offers a service analogous to that offered by PNS; nor is there a conservative investigative consortium to rival the CIR.

The absence of any effective competition makes it impossible to determine whether or not editors guard carefully against ideological bias when they work with investigative reporters. Editors and television reporters vary in their standards; some are more scrupulous than others when it comes to checking facts and squelching innuendo. But when they do reject an investigative story, or abandon a controversial inquiry, editors never attribute their decision to ideological factors. When an editor turns down a PNS story—or, for that matter, a Jack Anderson column—he invariably cites his uncertainty about the *facts* contained in the story. There are no rules—written or otherwise—that guide editors in assessing the role that ideology might have played in the development of an investigative report.

Certainly editors who use CIR and PNS material do not inform their readers about the ideological convictions that give that material its structure. How, then, can readers be protected?

Unfortunately, there is no simple answer—no dramatic solution. The only antidote to an ideologically flavored press is a counterweight—an adversary within the ranks of the mass media. Editors will not cease to carry information supplied by people who have a special perspective on the issues involved. How could they? Very few people develop a special expertise without also developing subjective personal views on the field. As long as reporters must rely on expert testimony for their background information, they will be at the mercy of subjective judgments other than their own. Those judgments will inevitably be passed along to readers, without any warning that the information is colored. The reader's only defense lies in the watchful presence of another, critical media outlet, which will pounce upon the excesses of its rivals. But no such watchdog can exist until the mass media outlets change their editorial policies, and begin to consider each other as objects for investigation, rather than simply colleagues in investigative work.

Chapter III—Notes

1. Better Government Association annual reports provide details of coverage accorded to all BGA investigations.
2. Fred Vallejo, "TV Barks Back at Itself," *Washington Journalism Review*, July/August 1981, p. 9.
3. Better Government Association 1977 Annual Report, p. 2. The *Sun-Times* coverage appeared in 25 parts between January 8 and February 5, 1978.
4. Better Government Association 1981 Annual Report. See also previous years' editions.
5. "Barroom Sting," *Time*, January 23, 1978, p. 32.
6. FIJ List of Grants and Books, in two installments: 1978 and 1978-1980.
7. FIJ List of Grants and Books, 1978-1980.
8. *Ibid*.
9. *Ibid*.
10. The Fund for Investigative Journalism, "List of Grants and Awards," 1980.
11. CIR Investigative Reports, 1978; 1979; 1980-1981.
12. Investigative Reports, 1980-1981.
13. Terry Pristin, "Cut-Rate News," *Columbia Journalism Review*, May/June 1981, p. 42.
14. Ron Powers, "Behind Mike Wallace...The Story of His Secret Weapon," *TV Guide*, December 19, 1981, p. 5.
15. *Ibid*.
16. "Exposing People for Fun and Profit," *Fortune*, September 7, 1981, p. 123.
17. *Ibid*.
18. Pristin, p. 17.
19. Powers, p. 10.
20. Cited at 1.
21. *Ibid*.
22. *Ibid*.
23. Frank Prial, "Coast Freelance Unit Thrives on Reporting for TV," *New York Times*, September 10, 1983.
24. *Ibid*.
25. *Ibid*.
26. Telephone interview, September 25, 1983.

27. Telephone interview with Robert Poole, August 16, 1983; see also The Reason Foundation Annual Report, Fiscal Year 1981-82, P. 5.
28. Telephone Interview with Ari Maravel, August 12, 1983.
29. Telephone Interview with Lowell Bergman, August 23, 1983.
30. Pristin.
31. Judith Anderson, "The U.S.—Poison Merchant to the World?" *Oakland Tribune*, May 30, 1981, p. 1.
32. Telephone interview with Frank Prial, September 26, 1983.
33. Telephone interview with Penn Kemble, August 19, 1983.
34. "The Gospel According to Whom" aired on *60 Minutes* on January 23, 1983.
35. The response came in innumerable releases and letters, notably a report entitled "The Gospel According to 60 Minutes," circulated by the National Council of Churches.
36. Telephone interview, September 26, 1983.
37. Reason Foundation Annual Report, Fiscal Year 1981-1982, pp. 5-6.
38. Pristin.
39. Powers, p. 10.
40. Mary Ann Hogan, "No Secrets," *Oakland Tribune*, July 15, 1981, p. E-1.
41. Prial. However, contractual arrangements are subject to change. As of May 1984, for example, ABC continued to work with the CIR, but on an ad hoc rather than retainer basis, according to Av Westin, executive producer of *20/20*.
42. *Ibid*.
43. *Ibid*.
44. *Ibid*, Prial cites a salary figure of $15,000.
45. Among the many compelling analyses, the best is Stanley Rothman and Robert S. Lichter, "Media and Business Elites," *Public Opinion*, October/November 1981.
46. Telephone interview with executive editor Jim Cooney, August 4, 1983.
47. Pacific News Service prospectus.
48. Telephone interview with Mike Cooper, September 23, 1983.
49. *Ibid*.
50. *Ibid*.
51. PNS prospectus.
52. Telephone interview with Jim Cooney, August 4, 1983.
53. David Armstrong, "A Thinking Approach to the News," *Columbia Journalism Review*, September/October 1978, p. 62.
54. *Ibid*.
55. PNS prospectus.
56. *Ibid*.
57. Armstrong, p. 64.
58. *Mother Jones*, March 1978.
59. PNS prospectus.
60. *Ibid*.
61. Telephone interview with Robert Poole, August 16, 1983.
62. *Ibid*.
63. PNS prospectus.

Chapter IV: Profits from Nonprofit Status

Whenever the U.S. Postal Service raises its rates, magazine subscribers can brace themselves for some unpleasant news from their favorite publications. Soon enough, the publications will write to them, explaining that the increased costs of postage have forced them to raise their subscription rates. Readers may groan, but at least they understand. After all, they reason, the cost of sending out thousands of copies of a magazine to subscribers must be fairly forbidding. What most subscribers do not realize is that actually, the most deadly impact of increased postal rates hits magazines elsewhere.

The economics of magazine publishing require most commercial publications to work constantly at increasing their list of subscribers. Even the best-loved magazines lose subscribers daily; if three-fourths of all readers renew their subscriptions when their term expires, the magazine has—in comparison with most other magazines around the country—done handsomely. Even among readers who would otherwise continue their subscriptions, some will move, or marry, or die. Some will fail to pay their bills, and the publisher will cancel their subscriptions. This attrition is predictable—in fact inevitable. Publishers do all they can to build up their readers' loyalty, and to minimize their losses, but they know in advance that their efforts will be only partly successful.

So publishers seek constantly to add new readers to their lists. And they do so by mail solicitation. A journal of moderate size might mail out hundreds of thousands of such solicitations every year. If only one or two percent of those who receive a promotional mailing decide to subscribe, the mailing can be profitable. Arithmetic comes to the publisher's rescue. If the cost to mail a subscription appeal is $.50 apiece, and a year's subscription costs $20, the publisher need only entice one out of 40 target subscribers in order to break even, at least on solicitation costs.

Actually, a rate lower than one in 40 might be a success. Among those who subscribe in answer to the solicitation, a certain number will renew their subscriptions at the end of the year—bringing the magazine added revenue with very little added cost. If the subscription list grows enough, the publisher can begin charging higher rates to his advertisers, pointing to the increased audience the advertisements are reaching. And then there are economies of scale in every area of publishing, most notably in the lower per-unit printing costs for a large press run. All these factors enter the publisher's calculations as he plans his direct-mail campaign.

Now imagine how an increase in postal costs would color the publisher's decisions. Postage makes up a sizeable fraction of the cost of direct-mail marketing. Since the cost of attracting each new subscriber has been calculated in great detail, even a small increase in postal costs can force the publisher to abandon his plans. Take the case of a small magazine publisher who has found in the past that he needs a 2-percent response from direct-mail campaigns to hold his publication costs even. Now, with an incremental increase in the costs of those mailings, he figures he will require a 2.5-percent response. But experience has also taught him that 2.5 percent is simply beyond the range of probability; there just are not enough potential subscribers. So, if he hopes to stay in business, he must generate increasing revenue from a decreasing number of new subscribers. There is only one option, really: He must raise subscription rates. And even that option is not so simple; if his rates grow too high, he will begin to lose subscribers. Once that happens, the magazine is doomed.

Readers need not worry about all these calculations—until they begin realizing that their publications might go out of business. Publishers worry about them constantly. From a business perspective, the direct-mail operation that brings in new subscribers is a constant, dominating concern. The costs of finding (and retaining) subscribers can mount up to one-third of a magazine's budget. By comparison, authors' fees are a relatively small expense. So an increase of even a few percentage points in that budget can imperil the publication's finances.

Now, turn from this general issue of magazine finances to a specific case: *Mother Jones*. *Mother Jones*, like many magazines of comparable size, predictably mails thousands of solicitations each year. But *Mother Jones* has one enormous advantage over its competitors: As a publication put out by a nonprofit organization, *Mother Jones* enjoys the sizeable discount in postage rates that the U.S. Postal Service affords nonprofit enterprises. As a result, *Mother Jones* can solicit new subscribers at a lower cost than can its main competitors. That, in turn, means that *Mother Jones* can charge lower subscription rates than can a comparable magazine working within the constraints of ordinary postal rates. And with lower costs, *Mother Jones* can reach a larger audience, generating higher advertising revenues and creating even more economies of scale. The extraordinary readership of the magazine—roughly double that of comparable ideological journals—suggests the benefits of this advantage.

Imagine, then, what could happen if *Mother Jones* lost that vital tax exemption. Subscription solicitations might be less successful, and rates would be forced up. Some old subscribers would balk at the new price, and cancel. Attrition, combined with the paucity of new subscriptions, would drive down circulation until advertisers refused to pay the same rates and printers refused to offer the same attractive deals. At the same time, *Mother Jones* would lose its other massive advantage: the ability to solicit tax-exempt contributions to offset its annual operating losses. Certainly *Mother Jones* would be badly hurt; probably it would be driven out of business.

Then imagine the secondary effects that would ensue if *Mother Jones* ceased publishing. America's most popular left-oriented muckraking journal would be gone, and with it would go the foremost publishing vehicle for investigative reporting. The Center for Investigative Reporting would be badly hurt; *Mother Jones* still accounts for far more CIR credits than any other publication.[1] And if the CIR fell on hard times, even *60 Minutes* could conceivably be affected, as CBS would need to find substitute sleuths to take the place of its CIR co-workers. And all this could come about simply because the Internal Revenue Service decided that *Mother Jones* was not a legitimate nonprofit venture.

As it happens, this is not mere idle speculation. From March 1980 to November 1983, *Mother Jones* and its parent organization, the Foundation for National Progress, were locked in mortal combat with the IRS over the issue of tax exemptions for the foundation and magazine. That struggle, as described by Angus Mackenzie in a 1981 *Columbia Journalism Review* article,[2] involved several different questions, including this most difficult one: "How is *Mother Jones* distinguishable from a commercial publication?" The case dragged on through several stages until the IRS finally decreed that *Mother Jones* could retain its exemption, noting that "profit is not a prime motivator in publishing the journal."[3] But the questions raised by that case are not rendered less intriguing by the recent IRS verdict.

If the definition of nonprofit organizations were simple and straightforward, many lawyers would be looking for other work. In fact, the Internal Revenue Service codes are a bewildering tangle of definitions, precedents, exceptions, and—most of all—questions of judgment. The history of IRS rulings on different organizations' tax-exempt status provides a jumble of different messages to someone seeking the blessed shelter of section 501(c)(3) of the IRS code—the section that confers tax exemptions on nonprofit, nonpartisan educational organizations. How much political activity can an organization undertake without jeopardizing its exemption? How much income can it generate before the IRS rules that it is, for all practical purposes, generating a profit? What is political advocacy, and what is education? Naturally, all these questions have been tried, answered, and tried again—often with different results in different instances.

In his *Columbia Journalism Review* account, Angus Mackenzie limited his scope, concentrating exclusively on the publications published under the shelter of tax-exempt organizations. That subject is broad enough in itself, as Mackenzie related:

How many nonprofit periodicals there are today is not known. About 177,000 tax-exempt organizations list their purpose as educational; many of them publish periodicals, but the IRS does not have a figure for this specific category. There must be several thousands—right-wing, left-wing, middle-of-the-road, religious, anti-religious, ranging in size from *National Geographic* (circulation 10,768,125) to *Mother Jones* (circulation 218,000) and on down to papers like *Big Mama Rag* (circulation 2,000), all educating their readers according to their own lights.[4]

Setting aside a few mammoth operations like *National Geographic* and *Smithsonian* magazine, *Mother Jones* is one of the larger publications in the nonprofit category. So in inspecting the books at the Foundation for National Progress, the IRS looked into the questions that decide the formula for nonprofit publication. How many copies of each issue are given away? How much advertising is carried, and at what rates? How are subscribers recruited? Is the magazine run in any way differently from the way a commercial venture would be run? Do the staff members have skills different from their counterparts in for-profit publishing? The IRS asked such questions about *Mother Jones*, and the answers raised some eyebrows. The slick, efficient subscription campaigns generated by the publication did not appear to be different from those in the most sophisticated commercial publications. When the *Mother Jones* attorney pointed out that *Smithsonian* is famous for its direct-mail marketing skills, the IRS inspector responded that he would be inclined to look skeptically on the nonprofit status of that venerable institution, too.[5] IRS agents have considerable discretion in these cases, and organizations like *Mother Jones* can only hope to persuade them—or their administrative superiors, in the case of appeals—that their educational mission still governs their activities.

While the economies of nonprofit status feed *Mother Jones*, helping it reach such an extraordinary number of subscribers, the same advantage puts Pacific News Service in a comfortable tactical position as well. Newspapers, like magazines, are high-risk financial ventures; every year sees the demise of dozens of small (and sometimes some large) publications. Every newspaper must seek out new ways of cutting costs without cutting quality, and one attractive option is the addition of syndicated features at bargain-basement rates. PNS, with its tax-exempt status, can afford to undersell its competitors, safe in the knowledge that tax-exempt contributions will compensate for its program losses. That, and the willingness of PNS correspondents to work for lower pay, make the PNS syndicate an attractive option for an editor fighting the budgetary battle. Especially before joining forces with the *Register and Tribune* syndicate, PNS gained another massive advantage through nonprofit postal rates. With two mass mailings each week, going to hundreds of syndicate subscribers, PNS' nonprofit status provided an enviable boost.

Needless to say, the advantages of nonprofit status have not been discovered exclusively by organizations on the left of the political spectrum. The Sabre and Reason Foundations, too, generate thousands of dollars in tax-exempt contributions without which they could not continue to function. But unlike *Mother Jones* and PNS, neither of these organizations could be considered as competitive with profit-making enterprises. Both are on reasonably sound financial footing (although the Sabre Foundation has cut back its investigative-journalism program), but each deals with a special audience, and (most evidently in the case of *Reason* magazine) a comparatively small audience. Still, the benefits of charitable status are obvious—perhaps even more obvious for these smaller, more vulnerable operations.

Competitors rail against these comparative advantages that tax-exempt organizations enjoy. But the IRS cannot take those complaints too seriously. For Congress created the tax-exempt status *precisely* to confer certain advantages on educational institutions. The only real question, from the IRS perspective, is whether or not an organization deserves those advantages—that is, whether or not the organization is really involved first and foremost in an educational endeavor.

Virtually any brand of journalism could be classified as an educational exercise. Newspapers exist to keep people abreast of daily events—certainly an educational function. Magazines combine more in-depth education with an admixture of entertainment, but any educational venture might involve a healthy quotient of pure entertainment. What makes nonprofit organizations different from their commercial competitors? The first difference, of course, is their disinterest in financial success. But even that is a complex issue. Nonprofit magazines cannot completely ignore their finances, or they will cease to publish. And many journalistic institutions are nonprofit against their own wishes; they try to earn money, without success. Newspapers fight a constant battle against rising print costs—a battle in which journalism has taken heavy casualties in the last decade. And most magazines devoted to the discussion of politics operate at a loss whether or not they are built on the expectation of profit.

In defining the scope of non-profit status, Congress (and, in greater detail, the IRS) has set several conditions. An educational mission must include some benefit to the public interest. Strictly speaking, an organization classified under section 501(c)(3) of the tax code must be a public charity: an institution devoted to furthering the public interest rather than its own institutional goals. A nonprofit organization need not be totally altruistic; it can seek to expand and preserve its organizational strength. But before granting it tax-exempt status, the IRS must ask whether the organization's *first* concern is a legitimate educational endeavor, qualifying as a public charity.[6]

To answer that question, too, the IRS has devised an intricate web of rules, definitions, and precedents. One clear rule forbids substantial involvement in partisan politics. An organization governed by section 501(c)(3) of the IRS code cannot devote itself to the promotion of any piece of legislation—nor can a publication sponsored by that organization. To some extent a publication can work its way around that rule with the familiar disclaimer that a writer's ideas do not necessarily carry the endorsement of the publisher. But even that rule is not forever applicable. If the percentage of pages devoted to such advocacy becomes too great, the IRS begins to grow suspicious.

Beyond the realm of blatant lobbying for specific, partisan political programs, the task of defining political activity is much more difficult. At what point does education become indoctrination? To avoid the appearance of censorship, the IRS takes a narrow definition of political activity. A tax-exempt organization is safe, generally speaking, as long as it avoids commenting on specific legislation, and instead propounds its ideology in general terms. Thus, for example, a tax-exempt organization cannot safely advocate a specific tax bill. It can, however, point out to its audience that tax increases tend to depress the economy. Or, if it (in its heart of hearts) supports the tax bill, the organization can point to the dangers of budget deficits. The implications of such "educational" activities might be clear to any intelligent observer, but the IRS will not intervene.

Still, even that technique has its limitations. The tax-exempt organization selects its issues, chooses the facts it presents, and marshalls its arguments as it sees fit. But the issues must match the purposes listed in the organization's charter, the facts must bear some resemblance to the data generally available to the public, and the arguments must be constructed so that a reasonable person, approaching the question from a different set of premises, might reach a different conclusion. There must, in short, be some discernible effort to educate the audience. The IRS does not presume to tell educators how to go about their pedagogical task, but it does demand evidence that some education—not rank demagoguery—is taking place.

Not many organizations classified under section 501(c)(3) find the IRS regulations terribly restrictive. They must be careful, and occasionally they can expect IRS auditors to question the way they conduct their activities. But with some care and some legal guidance, they can prosper in their roles as advocates and teachers. Yes, as advocates, too: the IRS regulations allow an organization to propound a set of views, provided only that those views do not constitute a pure political agenda. So in Washington, D.C., dozens of tax-exempt organizations participate in the political wars, pursuing the questions that seem most crucial to the success of their partisan cohort.

At least one such organization, however, does have some hesitation about complying with the pliable rules of the IRS. The Institute for Policy Studies, Washington's leftist think tank, boasts in its promotional literature that "the Institute stands on the bare edge of custom in the United States as to what an educational institution is, as against what a political institution is."[7]

Different publishing ventures are set up for differing reasons. Hundreds of academic and professional journals exist to keep subscribers abreast of their colleagues' work. Mass-circulation magazines exist to entertain and inform their readers. Literary publications encourage fine writing and criticism, while political organs speak for a certain discernible point of view. To be at all successful, a publication must know its audience, and stick carefully to its main field. By the same token, an organization active in the field of journalism— whether or not it publishes a journal of its own—must know where it stands in a highly competitive marketplace, and how its purpose sets it apart from competing entities.

The Foundation for National Progress does little except publish *Mother Jones*.[8] So when that Foundation, in its papers of incorporation, explicitly stated that its purpose was to further the objectives of the Institute for Policy Studies,[9] presumably the same purpose applies to *Mother Jones*. By extrapolation, then, one can argue that *Mother Jones* "stands on the bare edge of custom" in the distinction between an educational magazine and a political journal. The contents of issue after issue reinforce that suggestion. *Mother Jones* questions corporations and military agencies, but not counter-culture organizations or radical professors. The Center for Investigative Reporting, a prime purveyor of *Mother Jones* muckraking, raises concerns about the purity of the environment, but not about the nation's ability to defend against Soviet aggression. The Pacific News Service sketches the daily concerns of guerillas in Third-World countries, but not the equally pressing concerns of those who must battle the guerillas while attempting to keep a country's government afloat.

In choosing to emphasize these concerns, all these organizations are within their legal rights. They are playing the advocacy game according to the IRS rules. But it would be naive to assume that their investigations are motivated exclusively by the desire to increase the public's knowledge of political issues. The public is certainly being informed, but the range of issues covered is determined by prior, ideological concerns.

By way of contrast, the Better Government Association follows an unpredictable (and apolitical) pattern in choosing the targets of its investigations. A recent accounting listed these topics for the last few years' work: Chicago's "Deep Tunnel" sewerage project; defense contracting; Congressman Manuel Lujan; former Veterans Administration head Robert Nimmo; surplus government property; congressional caucus funding; home health care; unnecessary surgery; arson for profit; and the personal expenditures of Reagan Administration officials.[10] The unifying element in all these probes is the fact—or at least the strong presumption—that money is changing hands in large quantities. If the BGA follows a persistent ideology in choosing topics, it is the pessimist's view that large financial transactions can provide overwhelming temptations—for liberals or conservatives, Congressmen or military officers, corporate executives or union leaders. If all human beings are equally corruptible, then by following the trail of exchanged tax dollars one might encounter some surprising conclusions. An organization motivated by partisan concerns might suppress conclusions embarassing to its favorite causes. BGA exposes, however, have hurt both Democrats and Republicans indiscriminately, with plenty of grief left over for apolitical swindlers.

With a few years' experience, a capable investigative reporter comes to learn the tell-tale signs of corruption and incompetence. A full-scale investigation does not often lead the reporter to a conclusion radically different from the suspicions that put him to work. And since a prudent investigator never gives voice to his suspicions until he has compelling evidence, it is impossible to say how often any reporter or group of reporters reaches an unexpected conclusion. What *is* possible is to notice the road not taken: the potential leads that investigators apparently never followed up. In the CIR inquiry into the exporting of pesticides banned in this country, for instance, investigators apparently never looked into the question of whether those pesticides should not have been banned. In his book about the assassination of Orlando Letelier, FIJ author Saul Landau gave short shrift to the victim's connections with the Cuban intelligence network.[11] Such omissions do not necessarily detract from the veracity of the investigator's findings. They do, however, cast doubt on the motives behind such investigations.

That investigations are often motivated by ideological concerns comes as no surprise, however, since this is in fact the case in both profit-making and nonprofit journalistic outlets—especially magazines. Editors know that their readers have chosen the magazine for a particular purpose—presumably because the readers are content with the journal's editorial instincts. So the editors of magazines, especially political magazines, can indulge in much more open advocacy. (And, of course, the IRS' relatively loose interpretation of educational vs. political endeavors gives the editors of nonprofit, "educational" journals wide latitude in this regard.) But magazines pay a price for that freedom. Because their readers tend to agree with them in advance, and because those who do not agree are forewarned about the editors' own political preferences, magazine editors have less opportunity to change their readers' opinions on crucial subjects. More often than not, those who read will already agree, and those who disagree will not read.

However, when it comes to recruiting new subscribers who might share a magazine's political sympathies, there can be no doubt that a significant (and many would say overwhelming) economic advantage belongs to publications that enjoy nonprofit status. For it is this economic edge which sets off the chain reaction of more subscribers, larger press runs, economies of scale in production, and higher advertising rates. But at bottom, two disturbing questions remain: Are the operations of publications like *Mother Jones* really different than those of their commercial counterparts? Are the agendas of such publications truly more educational than political? It appears the IRS has resolved these questions to its satisfaction, at least in the case of *Mother Jones* for now. But these are questions that will recur as long as "educational" groups continue to operate at the very boundaries of custom and precedent on the nonprofit playing field.

Chapter IV—Notes

1. See CIR Investigative Reports, 1978, 1979, 1980-1981.
2. Angus Mackenzie, "When Auditors Turn Editors," *Columbia Journalism Review*, November/December 1981, pp. 29-34.
3. "Mother Jones Wins Tax Exemption Feud," *The News Media & The Law*, January/February 1984, p. 47.
4. Mackenzie, p. 31.
5. *Ibid*, p. 30.
6. *Ibid*.
7. Institute for Policy Studies publicity brochure (undated).
8. IRS Form 990.
9. Articles of Incorporation filed with California Secretary of State.
10. Better Government Association 1981 Annual Report. See also the annual reports of 1979, 1980.
11. Saul Landau and John Dinges, *Assassination on Embassy Row* (New York: Pantheon, 1980).

Chapter V: Conglomerates of Influence

The first cardinal rule of investigative reporting is to follow the financial trail. If an individual or an organization handles significant sums of money, the cash flow is certain to reveal something about the way the subject does business. It seems only fair to apply the same technique to the study of the organizations that sponsor investigative reporting. And it seems only fitting that the result should be a very revealing insight into the force behind some of those organizations.

In examining the finances of the organizations covered in this book, one is struck first by the relatively small sums involved. Only the Better Government Association, the Foundation for National Progress (which publishes *Mother Jones*), and the Reason Foundation surpass the million-dollar mark in annual budget, and the latter barely makes that mark.[1] For the others, the top annual revenue is closer to one-fifth of that figure.[2] Nor are the people connected with those organizations making enough money to raise eyebrows. On the contrary, the salaries are so low that any employee could earn a healthier income elsewhere. The lists of organizational expenses neatly match what one would expect for the sort of work being done; there are no unexplained figures that could represent questionable expenditures. If the statements of revenue and expenditure are any indication, no one is making a profit through these ventures.

83

With a comparatively small fraction of the sums spent in efforts to influence public sentiments, investigative reporters have compiled a very impressive record of achievement. The first criterion in assessing an organization's ability to persuade people is to measure its audience. By that criterion, each of the organizations studied in this book has a powerful impact. The Better Government Association reaches millions of readers and viewers through the stories generated by its press contacts, and thousands more through its testimony in Congress and elsewhere. The Fund for Investigative Journalism can take credit for several books, at least a dozen major articles in quality magazines, and scores of newspaper columns and editorials every year. The Pacific News Service reaches a potential audience numbering in the millions through its syndicate. *Mother Jones* circulation dwarfs that of comparable magazines. The Center for Investigative Reporting produces several vivid magazine articles each year, and its ideas work their way onto the most popular news programs on American television. The Investigative Resource Center provides the background information to support dozens of publications, formal and informal.

Even among the three conservative organizations, the product of investigative reporting reaches a substantial audience. The Sabre Foundation's reporting program has had impressive, albeit sporadic, success in placing articles with major journals. *Reason* magazine has a growing audience, and while its circulation cannot match that of *Mother Jones*, it is more than adequate for a journal of ideas. The Fund for Objective News Reporting has, to date, provided stories only for *Human Events* and *National Review*, but those publications reach an audience that can be measured in the hundreds of thousands.

In each case, the organization reaches a very substantial audience, and incurs only modest operating costs. Neither fraud nor inefficiency can be laid at the doorstep of these organizations. But a serious study involves more than an inspection of financial records. The next step, according to the canons of investigative reporting, is to look through the organizations' records, checking for suspicious patterns of behavior. Here, a study of these organizations yields some curious findings.

The Better Government Association works alone, teaming up with media outlets to make sure the investigators' story is told. One might ask why certain media outlets are absent from the list of BGA cosponsors (the local CBS affiliate apparently has never worked with the BGA, and it appears the *Chicago Tribune* has not worked with it in over a decade). But otherwise, BGA activities suggest no suspicious or irregular patterns of behavior, nor any inexplicable alliances.

The Fund for Objective News Reporting offers a different pattern, but one that provokes still less questioning. In the past, the FONR has reached very few publications with its products, but the connections between the FONR and its primary outlets—*Human Events* and *National Review*—have been too obvious to merit scrutiny. The FONR is a closely held operation, working within a small circle of conservative journalistic acquaintances. Until the organization succeeds in its efforts to place articles elsewhere, little more can be said about its patterns of behavior.

The investigative journalism program of the Sabre Foundation defies easy classification. The subject matter of the articles it sponsors has consistently followed the dictates of the organization's stated purpose, and the publications involved have been sympathetic to that purpose. But the Sabre program, more than any program similarly motivated by a discernible political ideology, has reached a variety of different reading audiences, and has shown its willingness to use widely varied approaches. In any case, the current dormancy of the Sabre program makes it impossible to draw meaningful generalizations about its efforts.

The Reason Foundation's foray into investigative journalism has served a simple, straightforward purpose: it serves the editorial needs of *Reason* magazine. Those editorial needs, in turn, reflect the Foundation's desire to broadcast the virtues of the free marketplace and the dangers of government power. No one who reads *Reason* could fail to notice this editorial perspective, nor do the editors make any effort to conceal it. *Reason* is a journal of advocacy, and its editorial policies follow simply from that fact.

Among the other organizations covered in this book, however, the pattern of behavior is striking. Each organization—the Fund for Investigative Journalism, Pacific News Service, *Mother Jones*, the Center for Investigative Reporting, and the Investigative Resource Center—supports the causes of the political left. Each is deeply suspicious of American corporations, American national intelligence and military agencies, and the goals of American foreign policy. Each contributes to the success of the others: the IRC gives research support to the CIR, which publishes articles in *Mother Jones* with the help of grants from the FIJ.[3] Above all, it is clear from other accounts that each of these institutions nourishes a strong relationship with a parent organization: the leftist Institute for Policy Studies.

After months of research into the workings of the IPS, Rael Jean Isaac wrote that: "It is itself an adaptation of the multinational corporation, and serves as an 'imperial' nerve center, with endless subsidiary operations that in turn influence and shape a series of ostensibly independent groups."[4] That description accurately describes the history of IPS relationships with investigative journalism. From the outset, the IPS was directly involved in establishing both Pacific News Service and *Mother Jones*; in each case, the IPS was the legal parent of the sponsoring organization (the Bay Area Institute in the case of PNS, the Foundation for National Progress in the case of *Mother Jones*). The Stern Fund (controlled by former IPS chairman Philip Stern) provided seed capital or other grants to the Fund for Investigative Journalism,[5] the Center for Investigative Reporting,[6] and the Investigative Resource Center.[7] Each organization contributes a distinct element to the overall effort, so that together the groups form a powerful opinion-molding influence.

Taken together, this consortium of organizations forms one coherent whole: a research facility (IRC), a team of investigators (CIR), a newspaper syndicate (PNS), a slick magazine (*Mother Jones*), and a funding mechanism (FIJ). With a combined annual budget rivaling that of a respectable think tank, the consortium reaches an audience numbering in the millions. In fact, without attracting much attention to themselves, these organizations probably reach as many readers and television viewers as some of the better-known think tanks in Washington.

To appreciate the ties that bind these organizations to each other and to the IPS, one must consider each group in turn.

The genesis of the Pacific News Service was sketched in Chapter One. Borne out of the Bay Area Institute—a declared arm of the IPS—the syndicate features six writers who are or have been fellows of the IPS.[8] *Mother Jones* is yet another arm, published by the Foundation for National Progress, whose avowed purpose is "to carry out on the West Coast the charitable and educational activities of the Institute for Policy Studies."[9]

The Fund for Investigative Journalism is ostensibly separate from the other organizations, except for their common dependence on the Stern Fund. But the pattern of FIJ awards leaves little doubt that these organizations nourish a special rapport. In 1978, the FIJ provided assistance to T.D. Allman, John Dinges, and Mark Schwartz, all of them affiliates of PNS; and to Craig Pyes and Suzanne Gordon, who worked with the CIR.[10] In 1979, the list expanded to embrace two PNS writers (Jana Bommersbach and Rasa Gustaitis), two CIR members (David Weir and Becky O'Malley), three *Mother Jones* articles, and another article that appeared in the IPS-sponsored socialist publication *In These Times*.[11] In 1980, the FIJ provided two different grants to David Weir, launching him toward the publication of *Circle of Poison*.[12] FIJ support helped Frank Browning, a PNS correspondent, to write two books: *Vanishing Land: Corporate Theft of America's Soil*, and *The American Way of Crime*.[13] In 1981, the FIJ provided help for Angus Mackenzie as he wrote his *Columbia Journalism Review* article lamenting the IRS investigation into the tax-exempt status of *Mother Jones*.[14] (Three years later a newspaper account cited a Center for Investigative Reporting story developed by, among others, Angus Mackenzie.[15]) And in an unusual grant not intended to help produce a publishable work, the FIJ made a donation to a libel defense fund for CIR founder Lowell Bergman.[16]

Mother Jones serves the collective enterprise primarily by publishing work the other organizations produce. But sometimes the connection is closer. The list of CIR publications includes a pamphlet by Dan Noyes entitled *Raising Hell: A Citizens Guide to the Fine Art of Investigation*;[17] the publisher of the pamphlet is *Mother Jones*. And the overlap between CIR and *Mother Jones* personnel is remarkable: CIR staff member Victoria Dompka has been a contributing editor to the magazine.[18] Mark Dowie has served as publisher of *Mother Jones* and as a director of the CIR.[19] Becky O'Malley has been a member of the magazine's editorial staff and a director of the CIR.[20] Richard Parker of the CIR staff has been listed as a publisher of *Mother Jones* and as the president of the Foundation for National Progress.[21] And Dan Noyes, one of the founders of the CIR, has also appeared on the *Mother Jones* masthead.[22] Noyes is also a founder and director of the Investigative Resource Center.[23]

The Center for Investigative Reporting, in its turn, has provided ample material for *Mother Jones* and other IPS outlets. In the years 1978-81 (the only ones for which listings are publicly available), the CIR sent nine of its 32 published articles to *Mother Jones*.[24] Two other CIR pieces appeared through the PNS syndicate, and one in *In These Times*, so that a full 37.5 percent of all CIR material turned up in publications explicitly affiliated with the IPS.[25] The CIR has received direct financial help not only from the FIJ, but also from the *"Mother Jones* investigative fund."[26] And in 1977, Pacific News Service granted $12,500 to the CIR, mentioning by way of explanation that "CIR has worked closely with the Bay Area Institute on topics of mutual interest."[27] By the estimate of both parties, the CIR uses the assistance of the Investigative Resource Center in more than 50 percent of its cases.[28]

No single case better illustrates the combined punch of the IPS affiliates than the book *Circle of Poison*, and the preliminary research and reports that brought the CIR a National Magazine Award. That work, undertaken by CIR staff members, was done with invaluable research help from the Data Center at the IRC.[29] The Fund for Investigative Journalism provided grants on two separate occasions,[30] and the *Mother Jones* investigative fund chipped in its share.[31] The award-winning article appeared in *Mother Jones*, as did the first sequels.[32] And Pacific News Service moved a syndicated column based on an adapted version. Thus, the five organizations worked together like one team, producing a blockbuster.

The instances of coordination could probably be multiplied, but the point should be abundantly clear. A small coterie of political activists has exerted a dramatic impact in the field of investigative reporting, by working through several different, cooperating organizations. Each institution retains its own identity, and follows its own agenda. But the net effect is surely pleasing to the parent organization, the Institute for Policy Studies.

There is, in this coordination of efforts, nothing illegal. But the proliferation of IPS affiliates, each growing in prestige and influence, does raise interesting questions about the independence of the press. Ironically, these questions were raised by a writer named Karen Rothmeyer, in a CIR-sponsored study of philanthropist Richard Scaife's publishing activities:

> By multiplying the authorities to whom the media are pre-
> pared to give a friendly hearing, Scaife has helped to create
> an illusion of diversity where none exists. The result could be
> an increasing number of one-sided debates in which the
> challengers are far outnumbered, if indeed they are heard
> from at all.[33]

*   *   *

The investigative reporter has tremendous power to influence public opinion, and thereby to affect the American political process. When investigative reporters unite to work collectively through alternative news organizations, the reporters' powers are multiplied. That power is multiplied still further when the organizations themselves collaborate, as they have, on carefully orchestrated programs of funding, research, writing, and dissemination, aimed at advocating left-of-center ideological views. By using the major outlets of the mass media to publicize their findings, these organizations imbue their work with a credibility—and impact—that individual investigators, acting independently, cannot hope to attain.

Investigative reporting is not, and cannot be, an assignment without ideological motive. On the contrary, investigative reporters tend to be cynical about the governmental and corporate systems they study, and ardent in their desire for change. By temperment, by training, and by tactical cooperation, investigative reporting organizations have become a powerful voice calling for radical political change. And the nation's major media have played an immeasurable role in helping amplify their cry.

Chapter V—Notes

1. Reason Foundation Annual Report, Fiscal Year 1981-1982, p. 18. The figure cited is for a projected, rather than actual budget.
2. IRS Form 990 supplies this information for the Fund for Investigative Journalism, Center for Investigative Reporting, Bay Area Institute (Pacific News Service), Investigative Resources Center, and Fund for Objective News Reporting. The Sabre Journalism Fund Prospectus includes full budget figures. Of course, the Journalism Fund is only a part of the overall work of the Sabre Foundation.
3. The best single source of illustrations for this interlocking network is provided by the CIR's clipping books, *Investigative Reports. Mother Jones* articles and the Fund for Investigative Journalism credit line make frequent appearances.
4. Rael Jean Isaac, "America the Enemy: Portrait of a Revolutionary Think Tank," *Midstream*, June/July 1980.
5. Rael Jean Isaac, *The Coercive Utopians* (Chicago:Regnery Gateway, 1983), p. 259.
6. Center for Investigative Reporting brochure, "California Center Offers Educational Services," by Daniel Noyes.
7. The Stern Fund's 1980 IRS Form 990 lists a $15,000 contribution to the Investigative Resource Center for its "Corporate Profiles Project."
8. The PNS publicity brochure gives capsule summaries of the writers' careers and institutional affiliations.
9. Articles of Incorporation filed with California Secretary of State.
10. FIJ List of Grants and Books, 1978-1980.
11. *Ibid.*
12. *Ibid.*
13. Frank Browning, *The Vanishing Land: Corporate Theft of America's Soil* (New York: Harper & Row, 1975) and Frank Browning and John Gerassi, *The American Way of Crime* (New York: Putnam, 1980).
14. FIJ List of Grants and Books, 1978-1980.
15. Jack Anderson, "Navy Infiltrates Group Opposing Nuclear Arms," *Washington Post*, Jan. 28, 1984, p. F19.
16. FIJ List of Grants and Books, 1978-1980.
17. Dan Noyes, *Raising Hell: A Citizens Guide to the Fine Art of Investigation* (San Francisco: Mother Jones, n.d.)
18. The names of Ms. Dompka and those immediately following can be found on the *Mother Jones* masthead and various publicity brochures.

19. *Ibid.*
20. *Ibid.*
21. *Ibid.*
22. *Ibid.*
23. *Ibid.*
24. CIR Investigative Reports, 1978, 1979, 1980-1981.
25. *Ibid.*
26. CIR Investigative Reports, 1979, p. 61.
27. IRS Form 990, Schedule A, Part IV, 4.
28. Author's conversations with staff of IRC, April 1983.
29. IRC publicity brochure.
30. FIJ List of Grants and Books, 1978-1980.
31. CIR Investigative Reports, 1979, p. 61.
32. *Ibid.*
33. Karen Rothmeyer, "Citizen Scaife," *Columbia Journalism Review*, July/August 1981, p. 41.

Philip F. Lawler

Philip F. Lawler writes on a variety of political, social, and religious topics. He is the founder and President of the American Catholic Conference, a Washington-based organization designed to give Catholic laymen a voice in the discussion of political and social issues that confront the Church.

From 1979-1983, Mr. Lawler served with the Heritage Foundation, a conservative public-policy "think tank." He served initially as Managing Editor of the Foundation's quarterly journal, *Policy Review*. He was later appointed Director of Studies, supervising the Foundation's scholarly research. Formerly, Mr. Lawler edited *Prospect* magazine in Princeton, New Jersey.

A Boston native, Mr. Lawler graduated with honors from Harvard College in 1972, and pursued graduate studies in political philosophy at the University of Chicago. He continues to work in the academic community as Program Director of the International Foundation for Human Sciences, while serving on the editorial boards of *Catholicism in Crisis* and the *Hillsdale Review*.

Mr. Lawler is the author of *The Ultimate Weapon* and *Coughing in Ink*. He is the editor of *Justice and War in the Nuclear Age*, and has produced several monographs on Catholic social teachings. His essays and book reviews have appeared in dozens of journals, such as *Policy Review*, *American Spectator*, *Catholicism in Crisis*, *National Review*, and *Modern Age*. Over 100 newspapers around the United States have used his editorial columns, among them the *Washington Post* and *Los Angeles Times*.

The Media Institute

The Media Institute is a nonprofit, tax-exempt research organization supported by a wide range of foundations, corporations, associations and individuals. The Institute has published a number of studies analyzing media coverage of major public policy issues, and sponsors other programs related to business/media relations, the new technologies, and communications issues, both domestic and international.

Media in Society Series. General Editor: Richard T. Kaplar.
Production: David P. Taggart.

The Media Institute • 3017 M St., N.W. • Washington, D.C. 20007 • 202-298-7512